FOR ORGANS, PIANOS & ELECTRONIC KEYBOARDS

E-Z PLAY TODAY

3

CONTEMPORARY Disney

30 FAVORITE SONGS

Characters and Artwork © Disney Enterprises, Inc./Pixar

ISBN 978-1-5400-3682-7

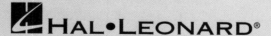

Visit Hal Leonard Online at
www.halleonard.com

E-Z PLAY ® TODAY Music Notation © 1975 HAL LEONARD CORPORATION
E-Z PLAY and EASY ELECTRONIC KEYBOARD MUSIC are registered trademarks of HAL LEONARD CORPORATION.

Contact Us:
Hal Leonard
7777 West Bluemound Road
Milwaukee, WI 53213
Email: info@halleonard.com

In Europe contact:
Hal Leonard Europe Limited
Distribution Centre, Newmarket Road
Bury St Edmunds, Suffolk, IP33 3YB
Email: info@halleonardeurope.com

In Australia contact:
Hal Leonard Australia Pty. Ltd.
4 Lentara Court
Cheltenham, Victoria, 3192 Australia
Email: info@halleonard.com.au

Almost There
from THE PRINCESS AND THE FROG

Registration 3
Rhythm: Slow Swing

Music and Lyrics by
Randy Newman

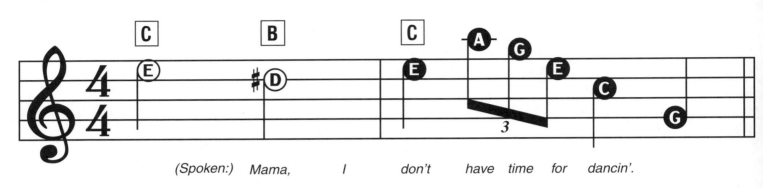

(Spoken:) Mama, I don't have time for dancin'.

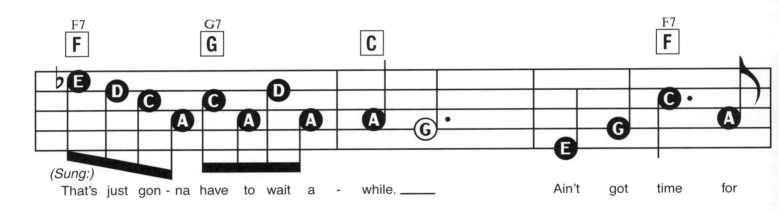

(Sung:) That's just gon-na have to wait a - while. _____ Ain't got time for

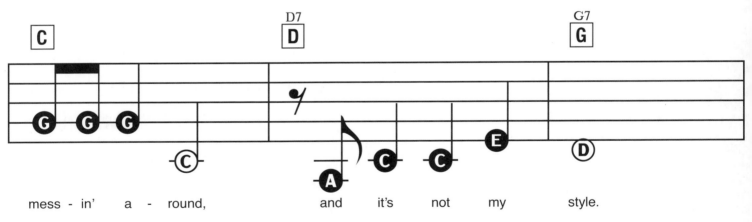

mess - in' a - round, and it's not my style.

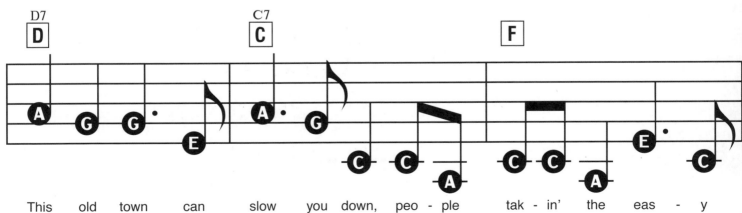

This old town can slow you down, peo - ple tak - in' the eas - y

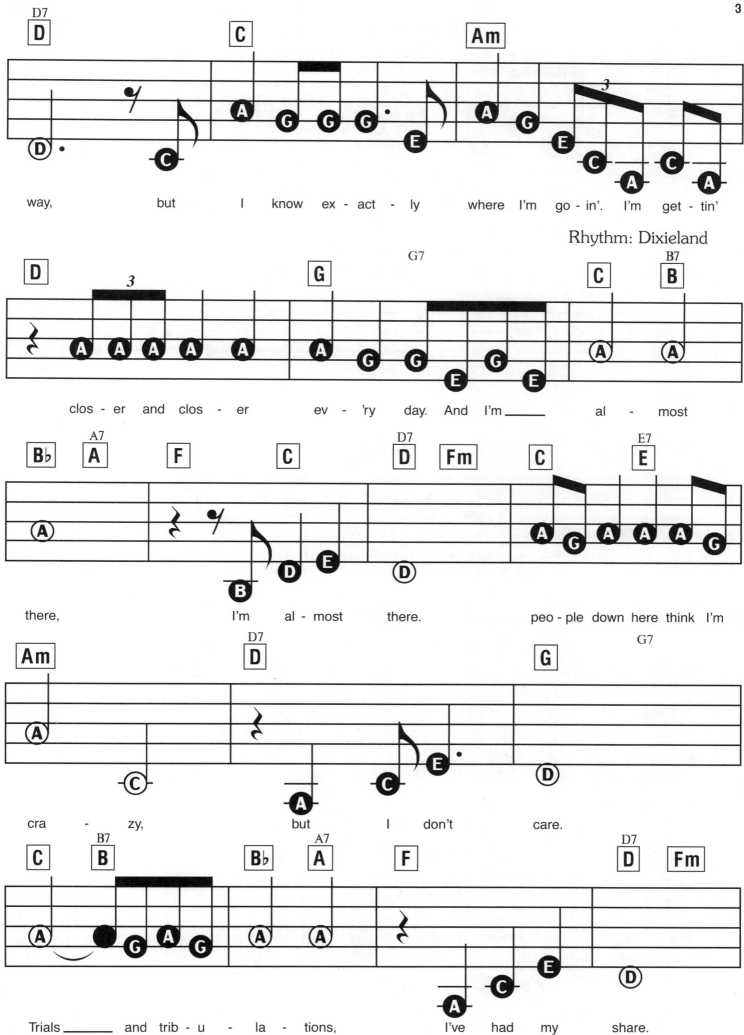

Rhythm: Dixieland

way, but I know ex - act - ly where I'm go - in'. I'm get - tin'

clos - er and clos - er ev - 'ry day. And I'm _____ al - most

there, I'm al - most there. peo - ple down here think I'm

cra - zy, but I don't care.

Trials _____ and trib - u - la - tions, I've had my share.

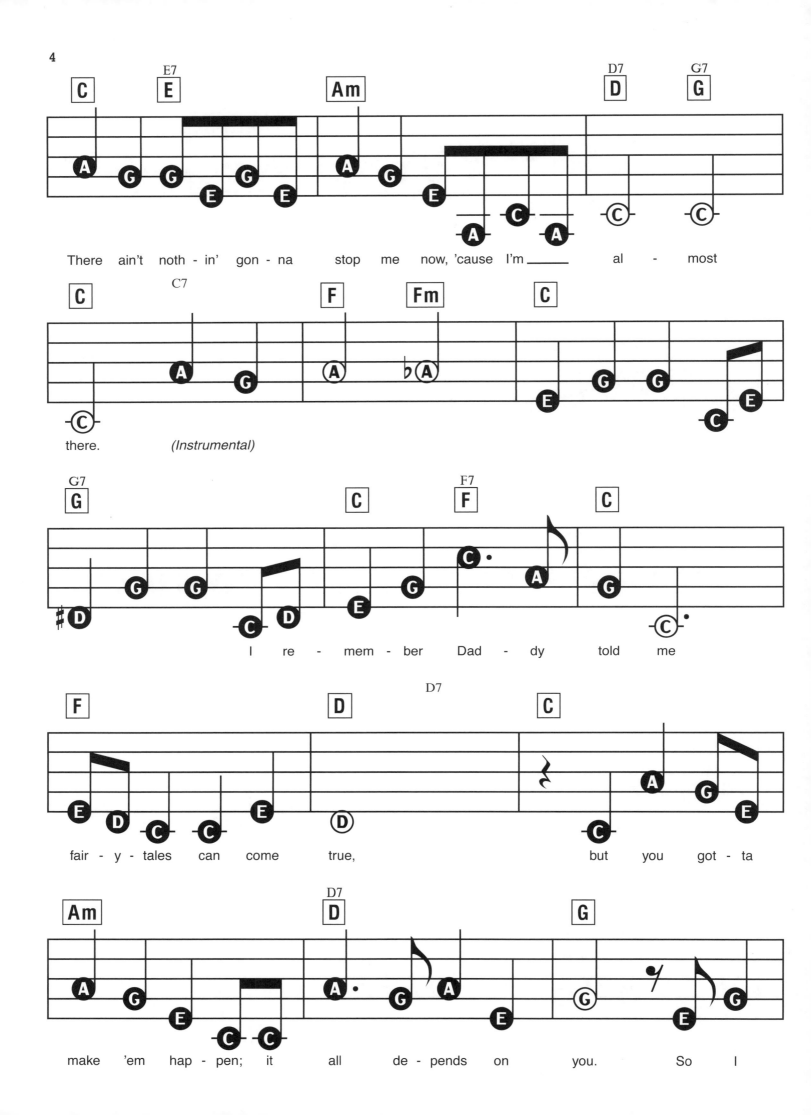

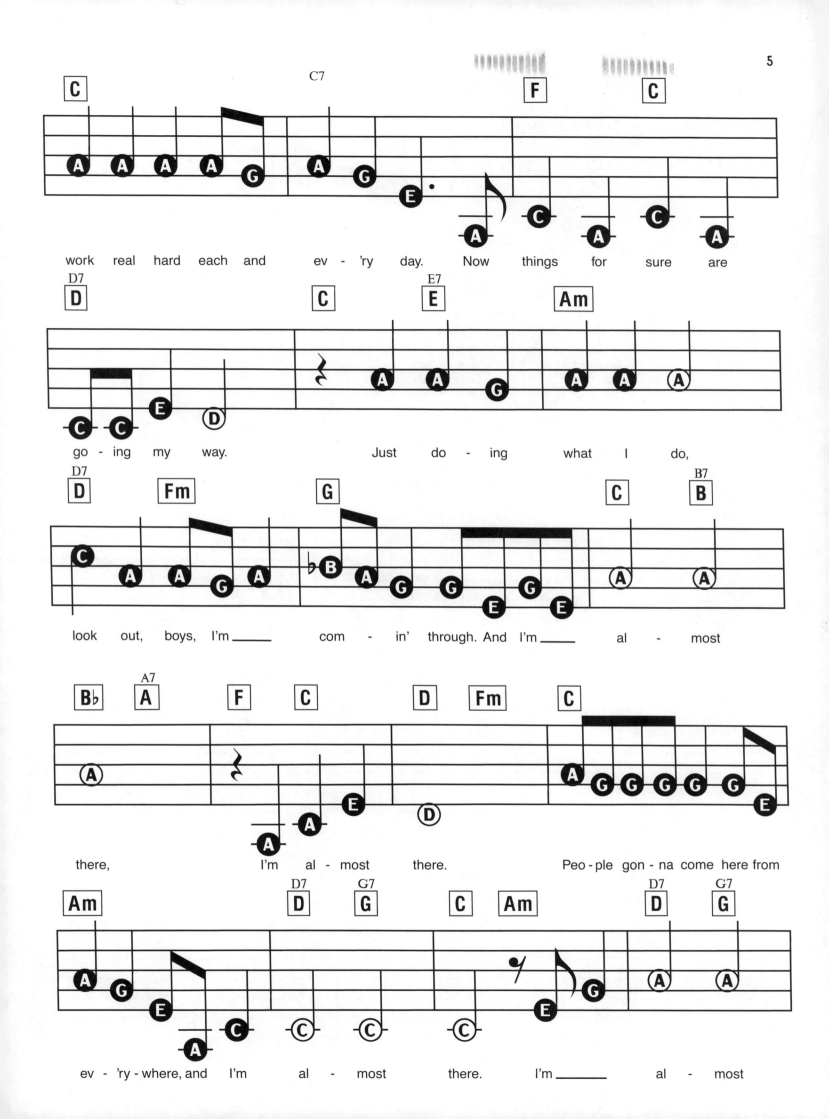

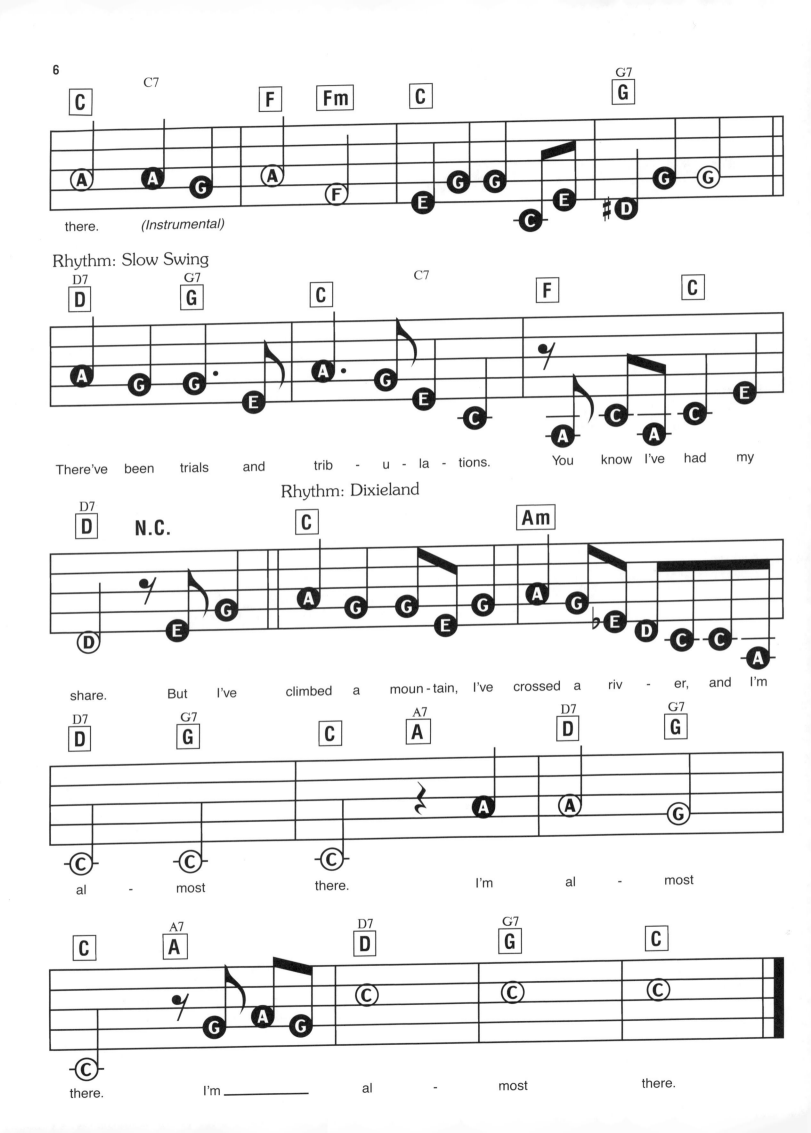

6

Can You Feel the Love Tonight
from THE LION KING

Registration 1
Rhythm: Ballad or Pops

Music by Elton John
Lyrics by Tim Rice

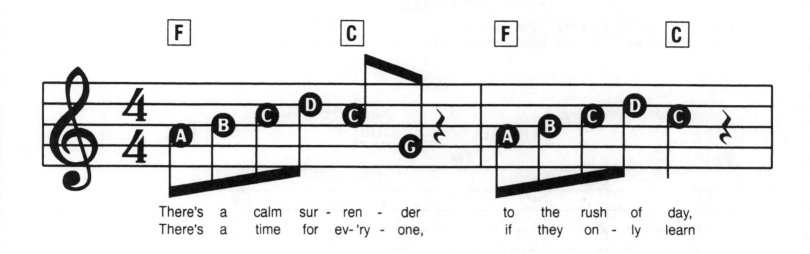

There's a calm sur-ren-der   to the rush of day,
There's a time for ev-'ry-one,   if they on-ly learn

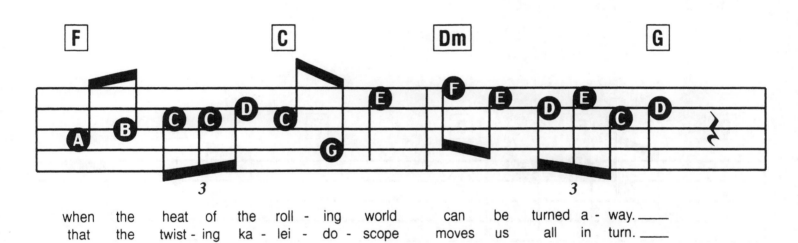

when the heat of the roll-ing world   can be turned a-way. ___
that the twist-ing ka-lei-do-scope   moves us all in turn. ___

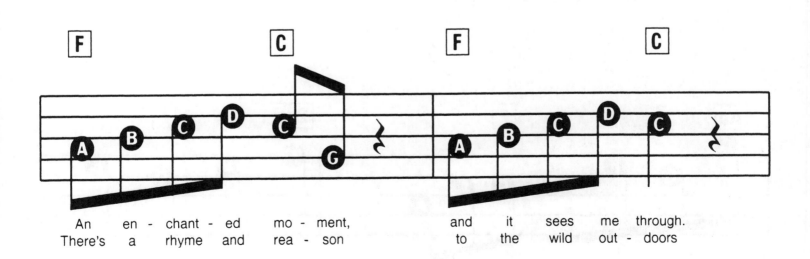

An en-chant-ed mo-ment,   and it sees me through.
There's a rhyme and rea-son   to the wild out-doors

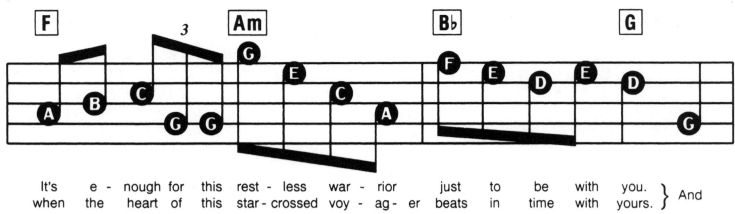

It's e - nough for this rest - less war - rior just to be with you. } And
when the heart of this star - crossed voy - ag - er beats in time with yours.

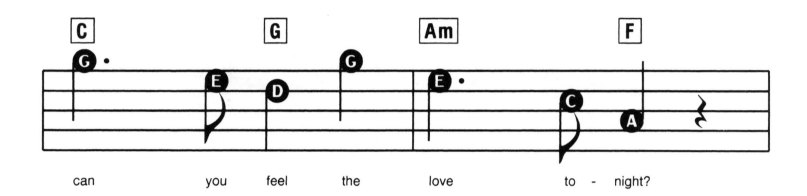

can you feel the love to - night?

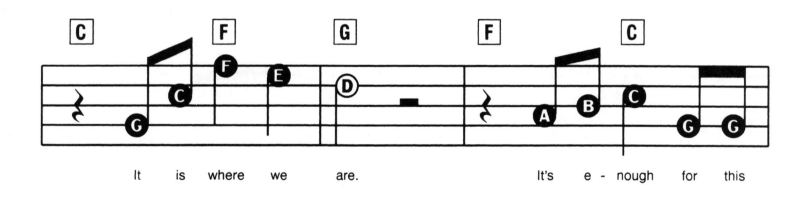

It is where we are. It's e - nough for this

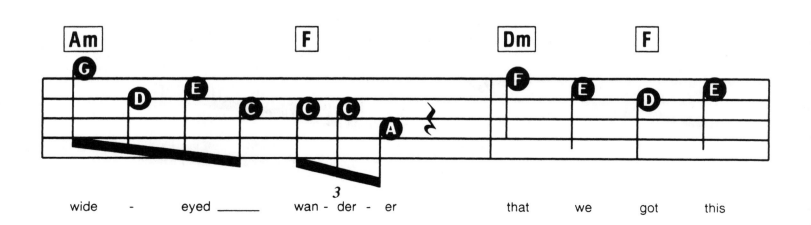

wide - eyed _____ wan - der - er that we got this

Beauty and the Beast
from BEAUTY AND THE BEAST

Registration 1
Rhythm: Ballad

Music by Alan Menken
Lyrics by Howard Ashman

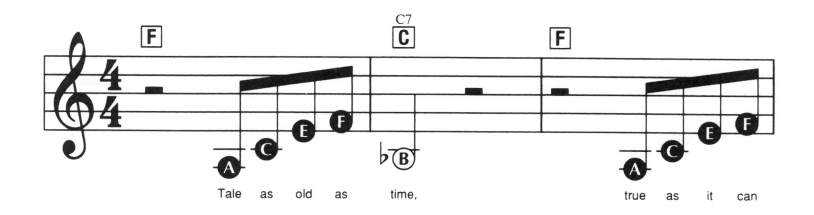

Tale as old as time, true as it can

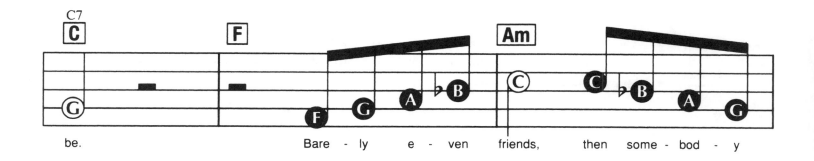

be. Bare - ly e - ven friends, then some - bod - y

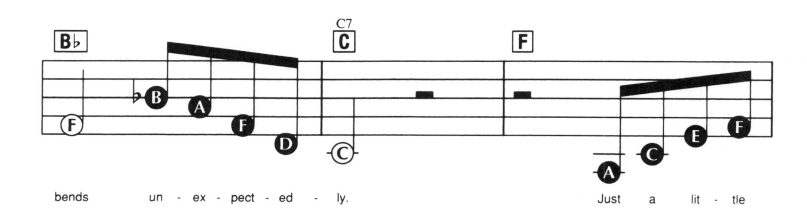

bends un - ex - pect - ed - ly. Just a lit - tle

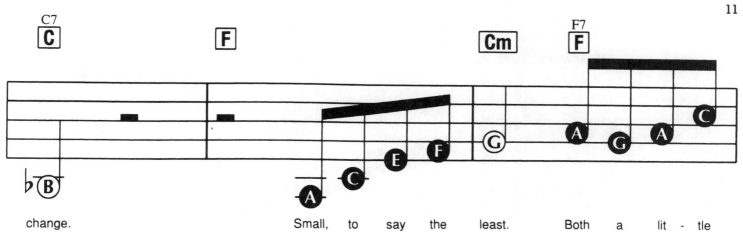

change. Small, to say the least. Both a lit - tle

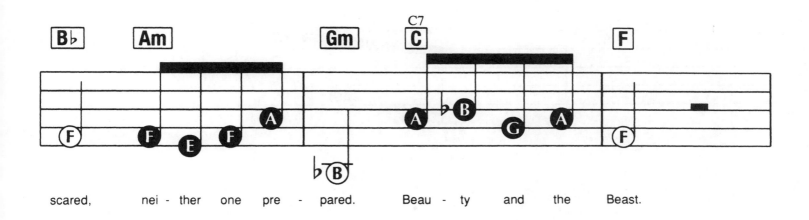

scared, nei - ther one pre - pared. Beau - ty and the Beast.

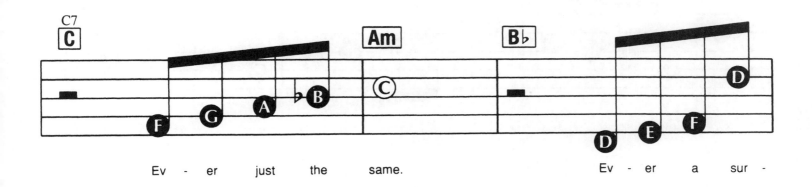

Ev - er just the same. Ev - er a sur -

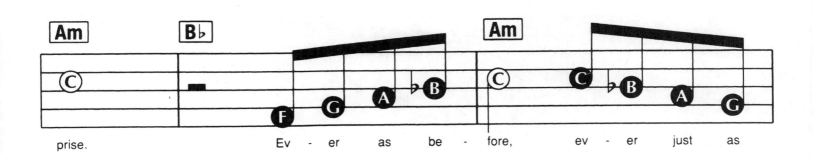

prise. Ev - er as be - fore, ev - er just as

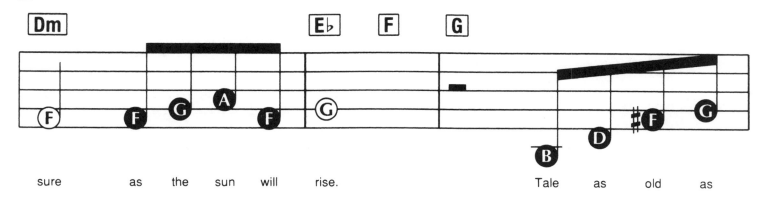

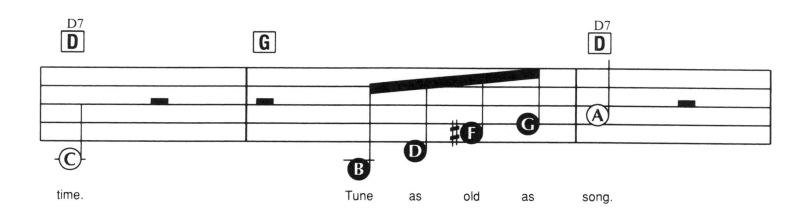

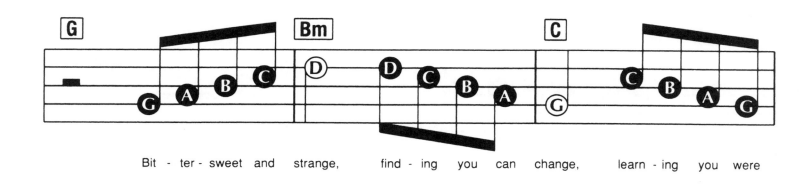

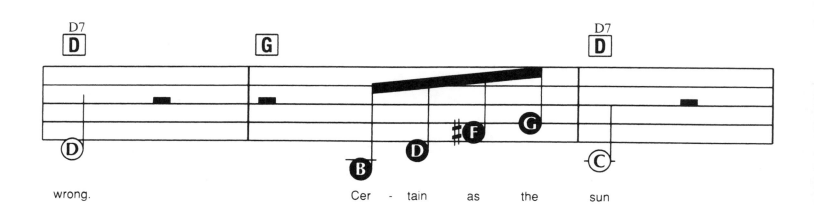

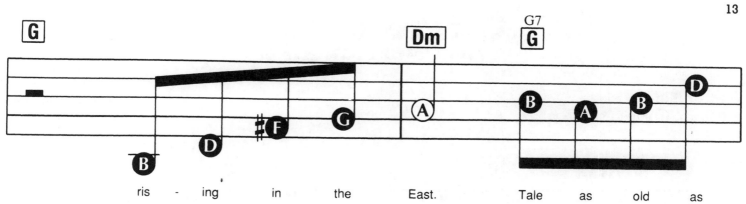

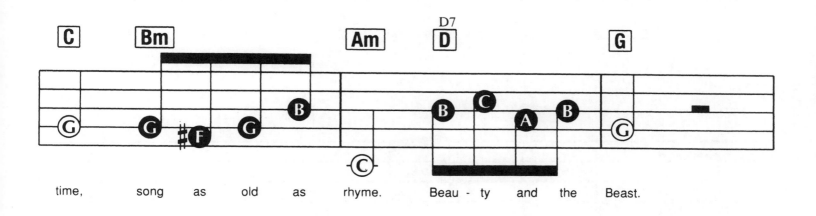

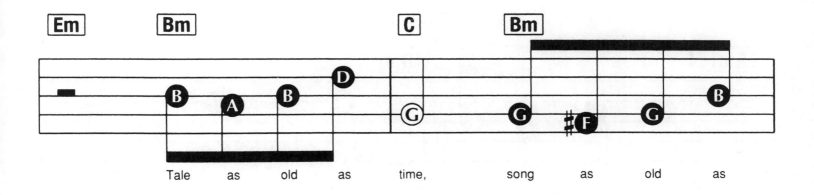

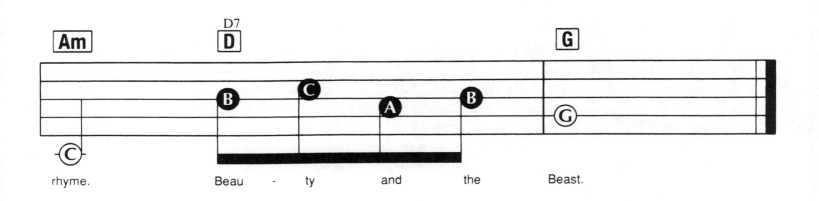

Circle of Life
from THE LION KING

Registration 2
Rhythm: Calypso or Reggae

Music by Elton John
Lyrics by Tim Rice

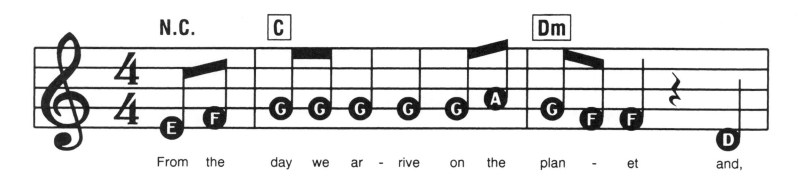

From the day we ar - rive on the plan - et and,

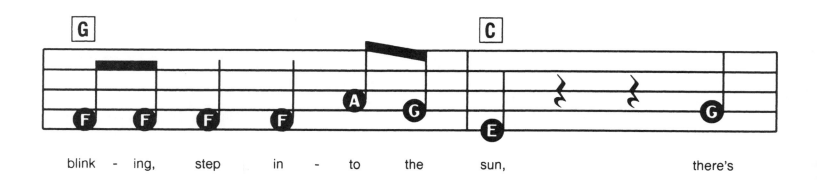

blink - ing, step in - to the sun, there's

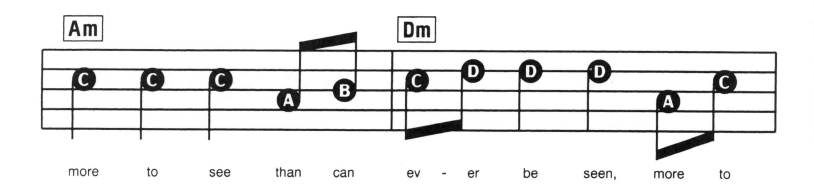

more to see than can ev - er be seen, more to

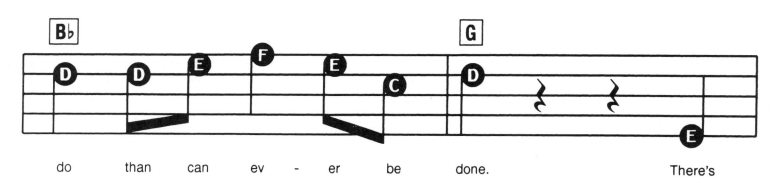

do than can ev - er be done. There's

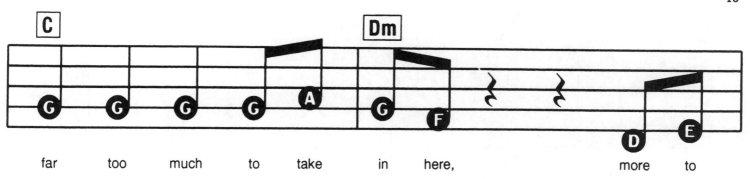

far   too   much   to   take   in   here,   more   to

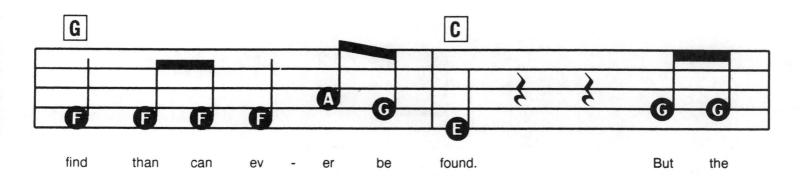

find   than   can   ev - er   be   found.   But   the

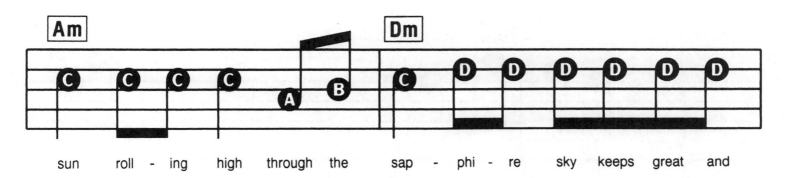

sun   roll - ing   high   through   the   sap - phi - re   sky   keeps   great   and

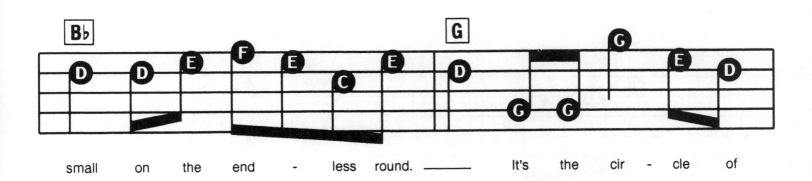

small   on   the   end - less   round. _____   It's   the   cir - cle   of

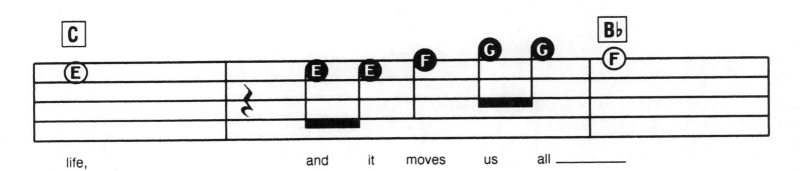

life,   and   it   moves   us   all _____

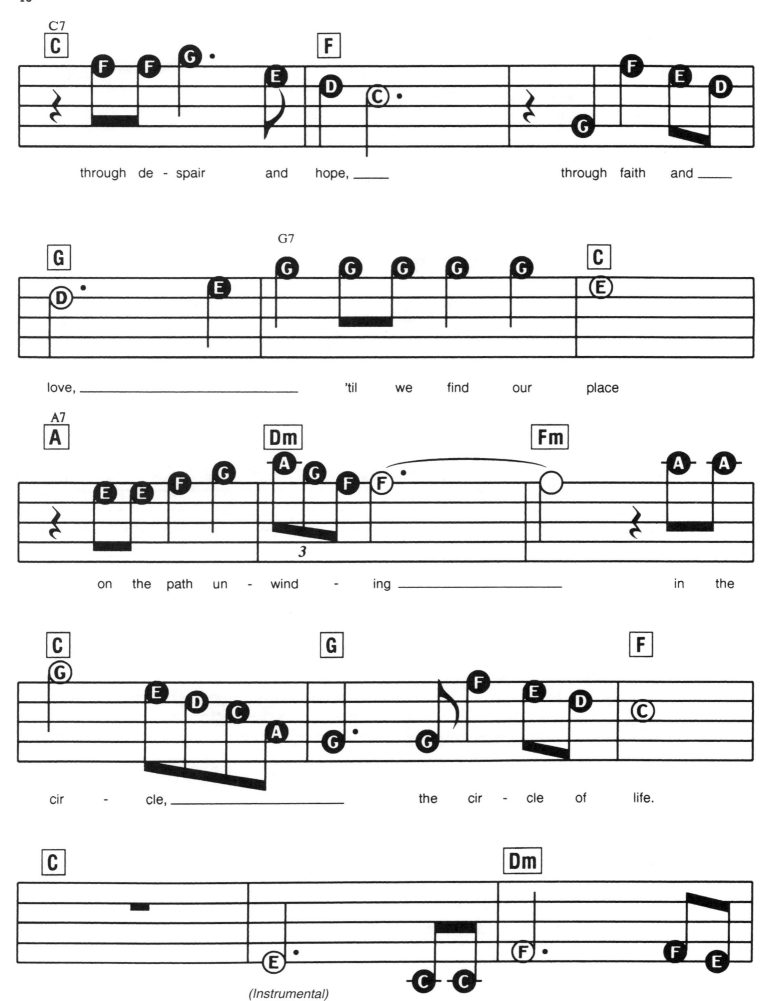

through de - spair and hope, _____ through faith and _____

love, _____ 'til we find our place

on the path un - wind - ing _____ in the

cir - cle, _____ the cir - cle of life.

(Instrumental)

It's the cir - cle of life,

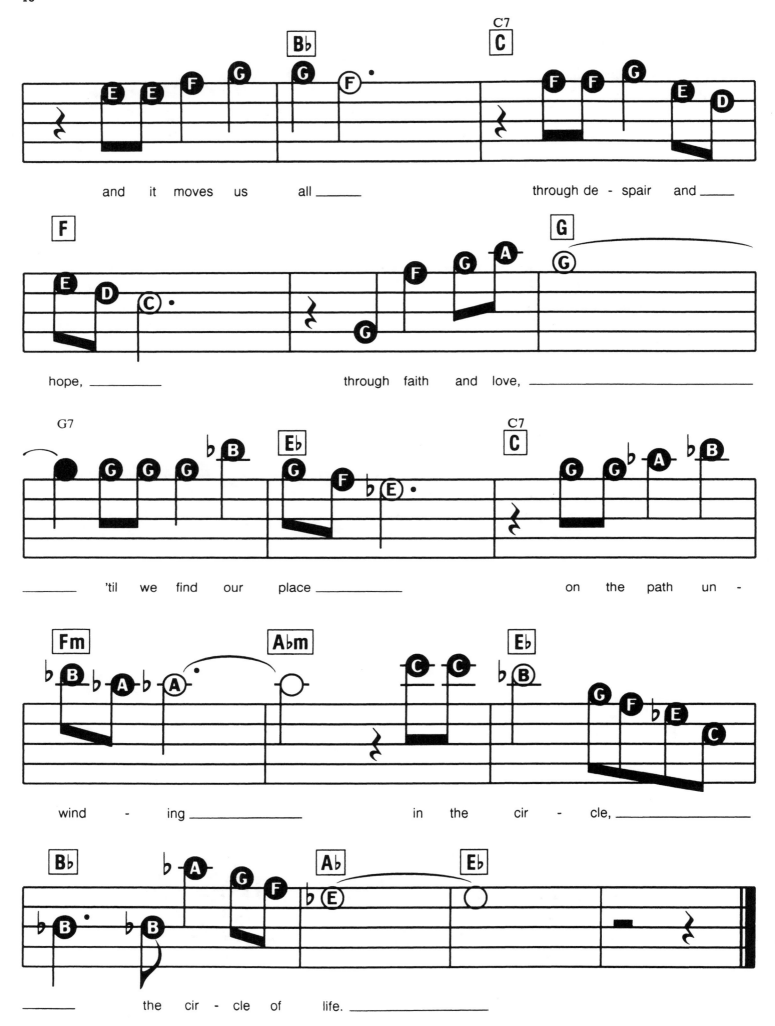

Colors of the Wind
from POCAHONTAS

Registration 5
Rhythm: None

Music by Alan Menken
Lyrics by Stephen Schwartz

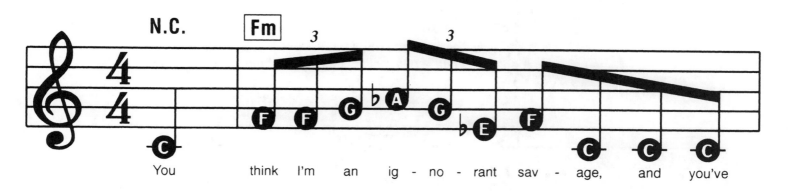

You think I'm an ig - no - rant sav - age, and you've

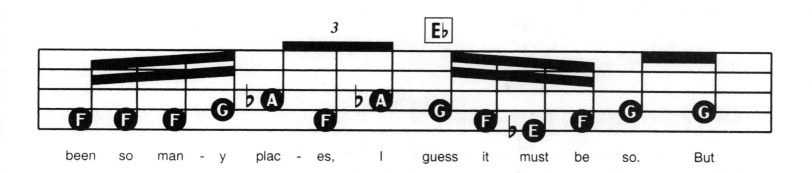

been so man - y plac - es, I guess it must be so. But

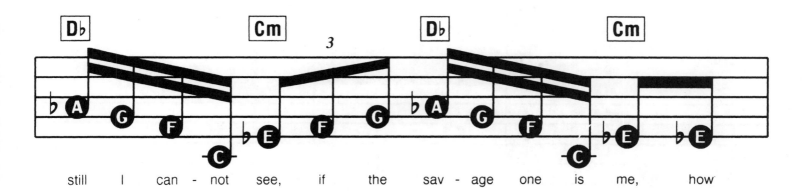

still I can - not see, if the sav - age one is me, how

Rhythm: Rock or 8-Beat

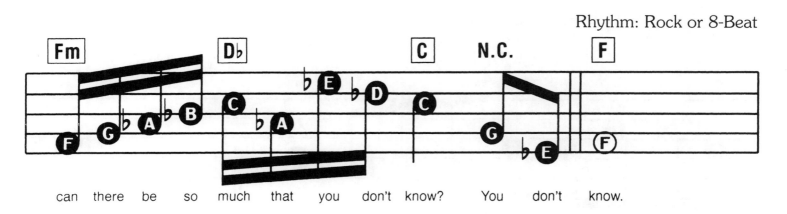

can there be so much that you don't know? You don't know.

20

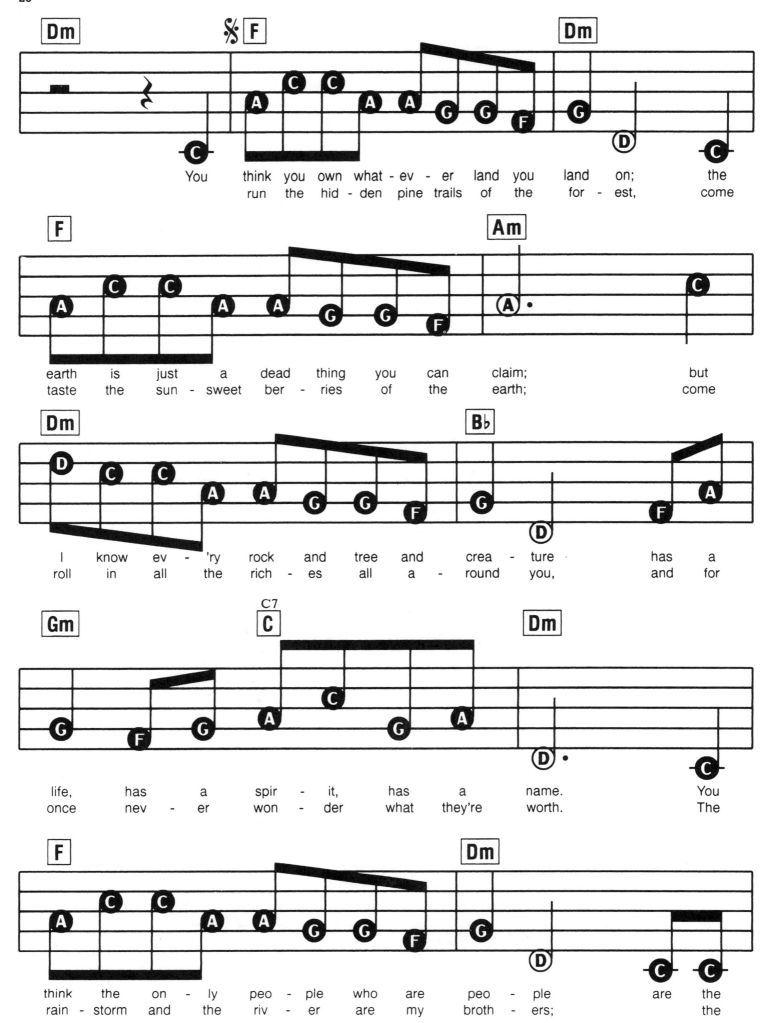

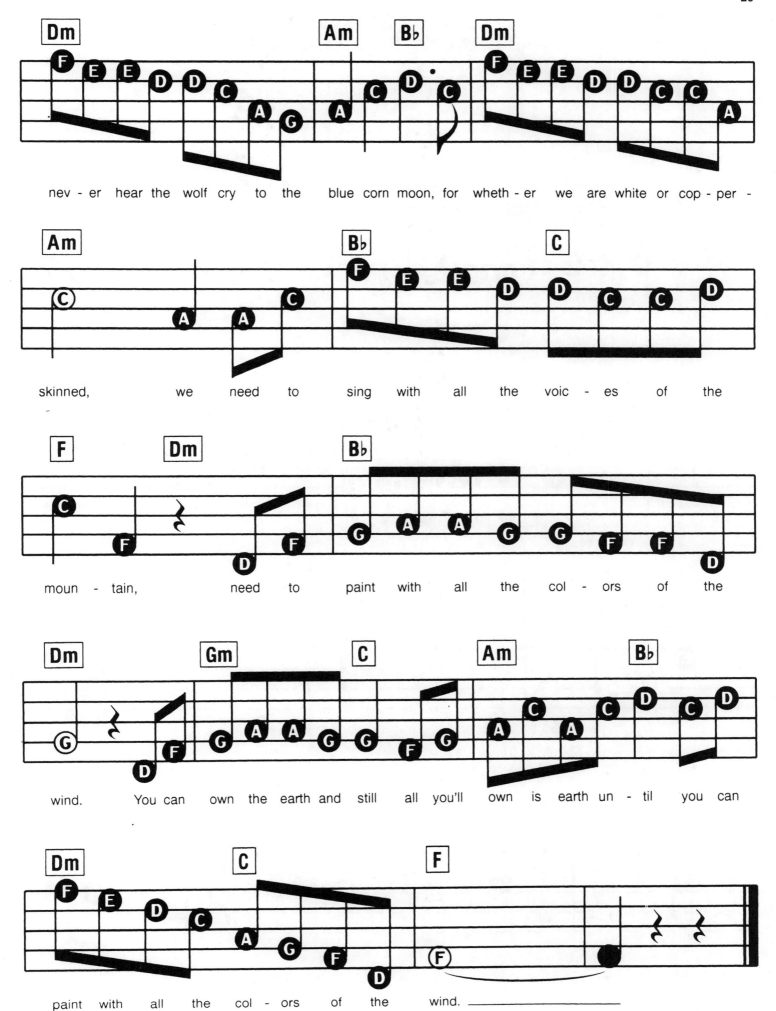

23

24

Evermore
from BEAUTY AND THE BEAST

Registration 2
Rhythm: Ballad

Music by Alan Menken
Lyrics by Tim Rice

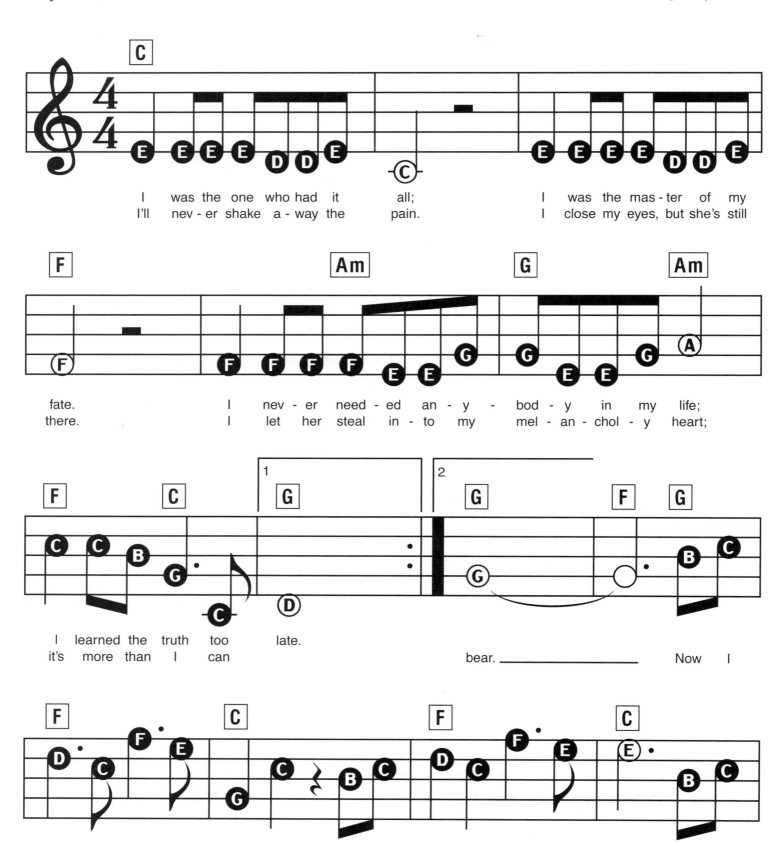

I was the one who had it all; I was the mas-ter of my
I'll nev-er shake a-way the pain. I close my eyes, but she's still

fate. I nev-er need-ed an-y-bod-y in my life;
there. I let her steal in-to my mel-an-chol-y heart;

I learned the truth too late.
it's more than I can bear. _____ Now I

know she'll nev-er leave me, e-ven as she runs a-way. She will

© 2017 Wonderland Music Company, Inc.
All Rights Reserved. Used by Permission.

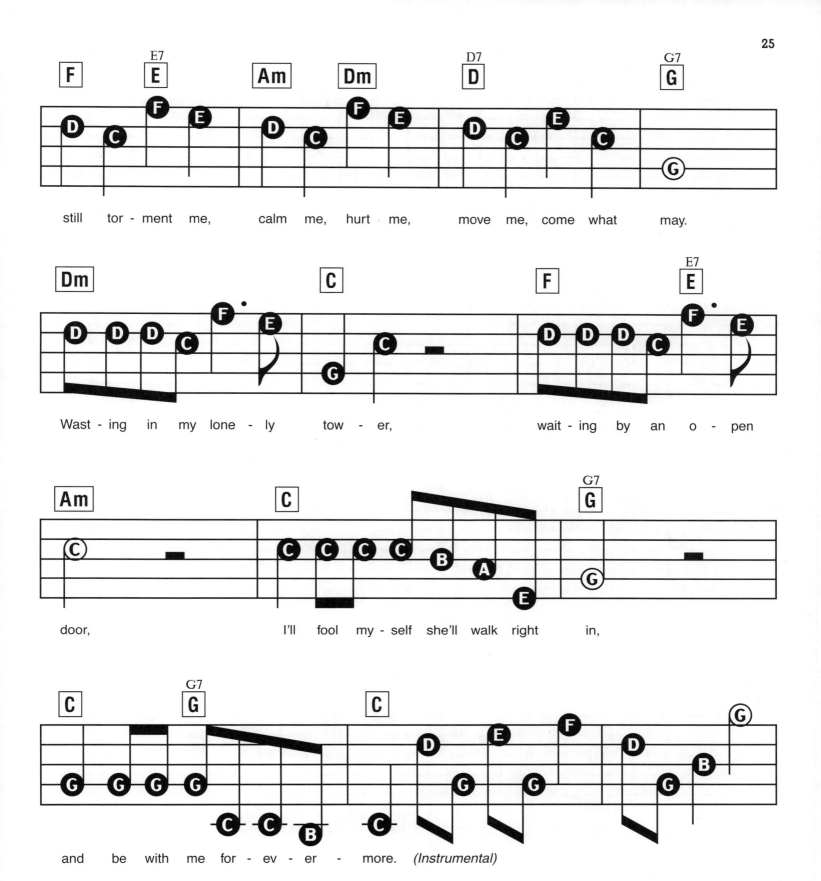

still tor - ment me, calm me, hurt me, move me, come what may.

Wast - ing in my lone - ly tow - er, wait - ing by an o - pen

door, I'll fool my - self she'll walk right in,

and be with me for - ev - er - more. *(Instrumental)*

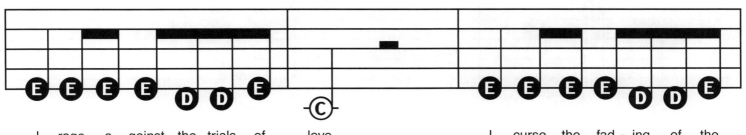

I rage a - gainst the trials of love. I curse the fad - ing of the

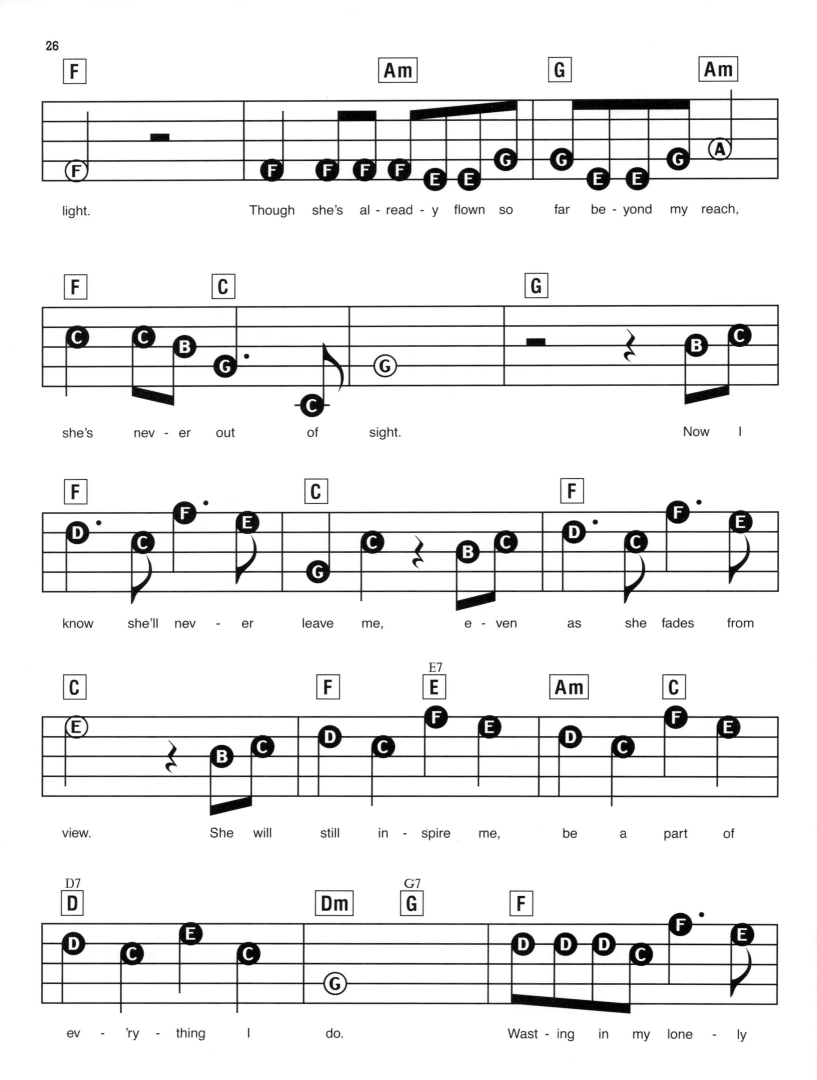

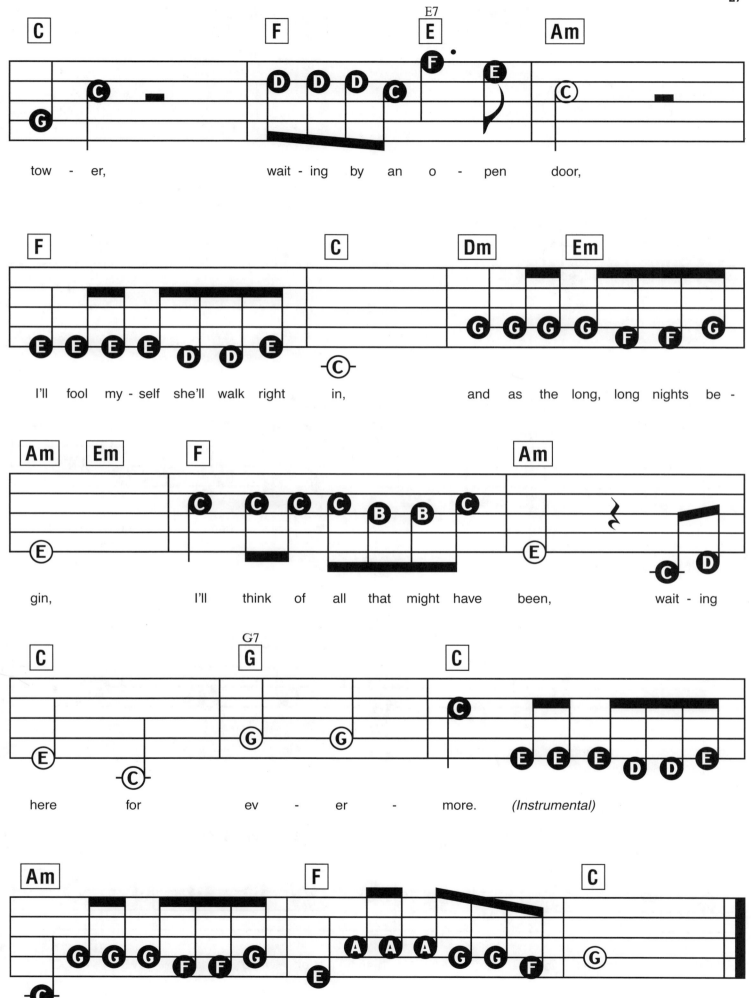

Friend Like Me
from ALADDIN

Registration 1
Rhythm: Polka or March

Music by Alan Menken
Lyrics by Howard Ashman

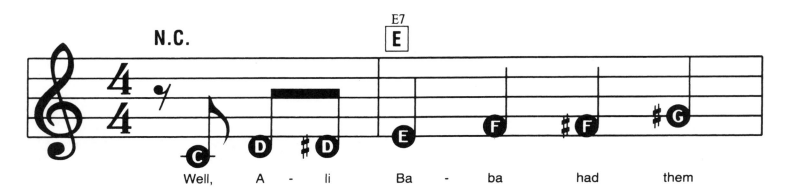

Well, A - li Ba - ba had them

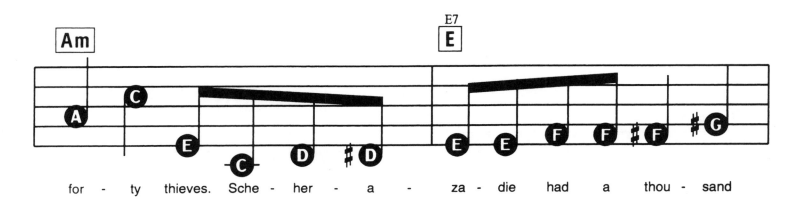

for - ty thieves. Sche - her - a - za - die had a thou - sand

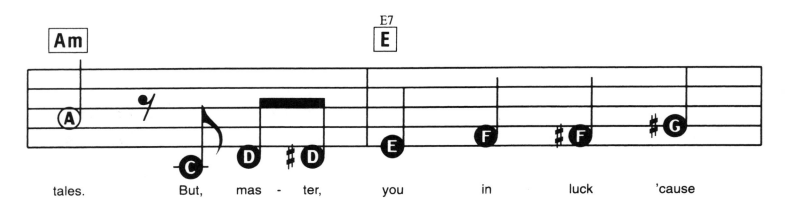

tales. But, mas - ter, you in luck 'cause

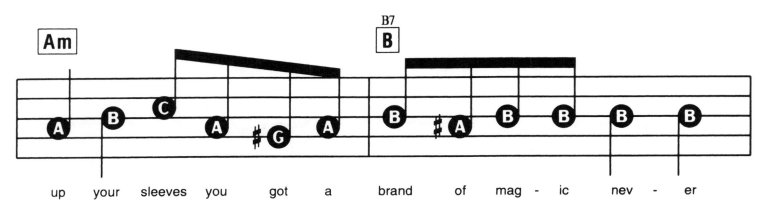

up your sleeves you got a brand of mag - ic nev - er

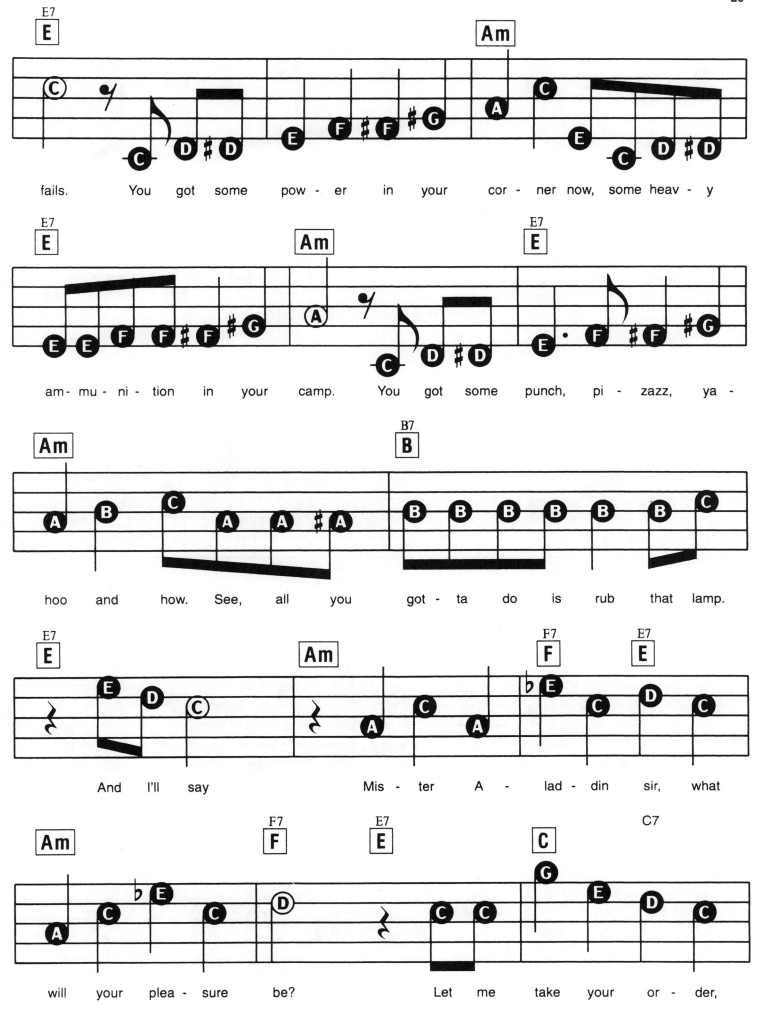

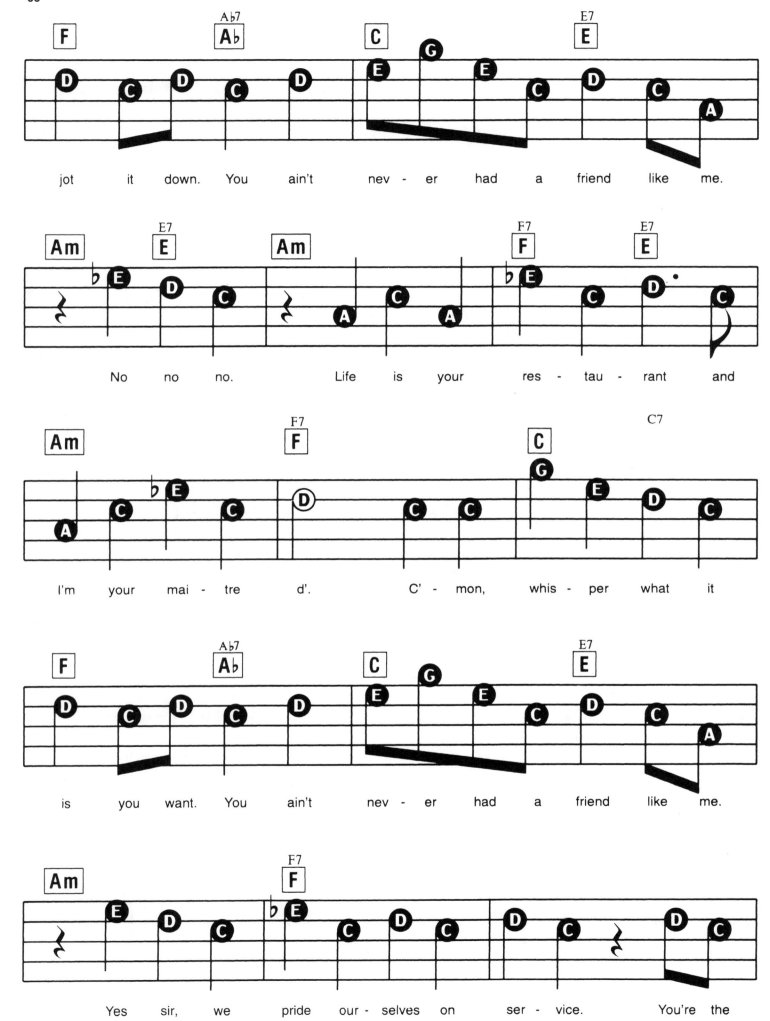

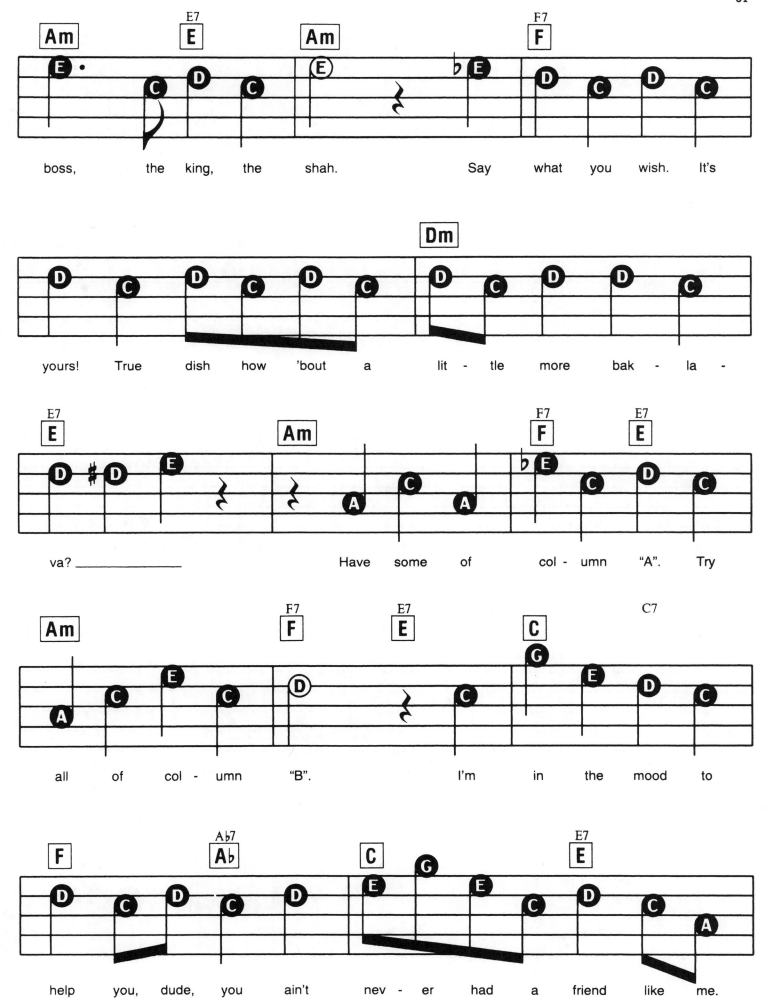

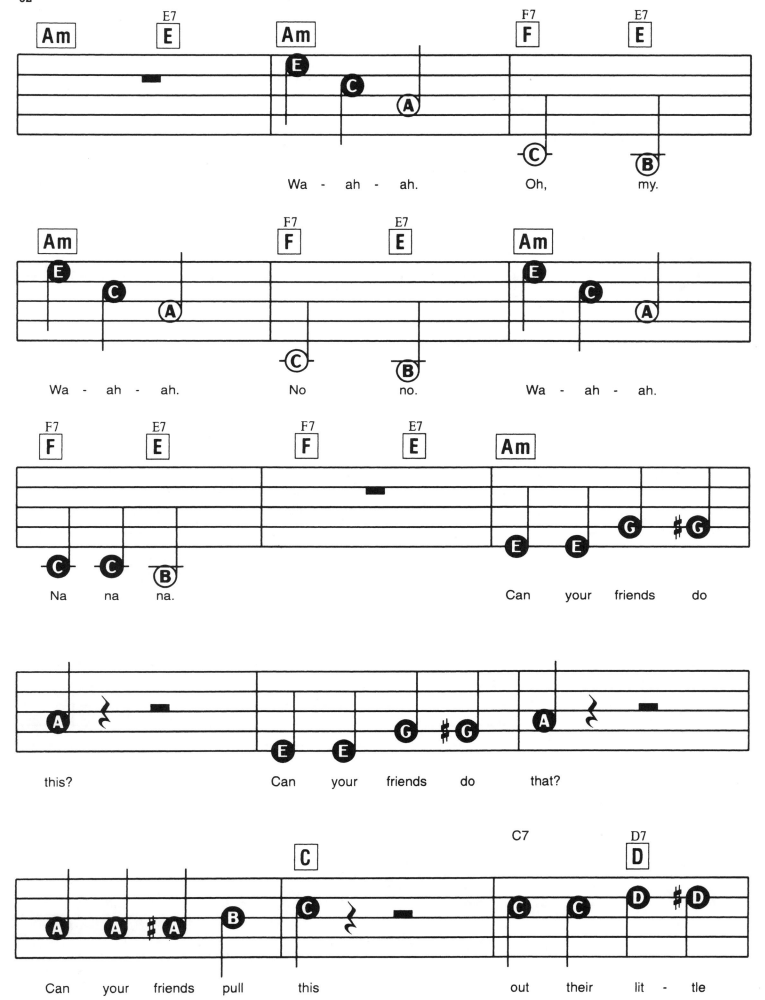

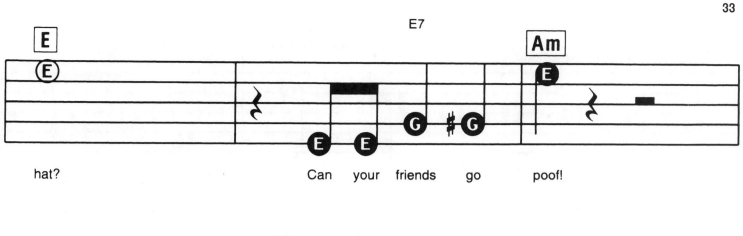

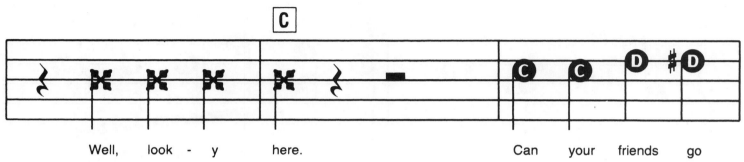

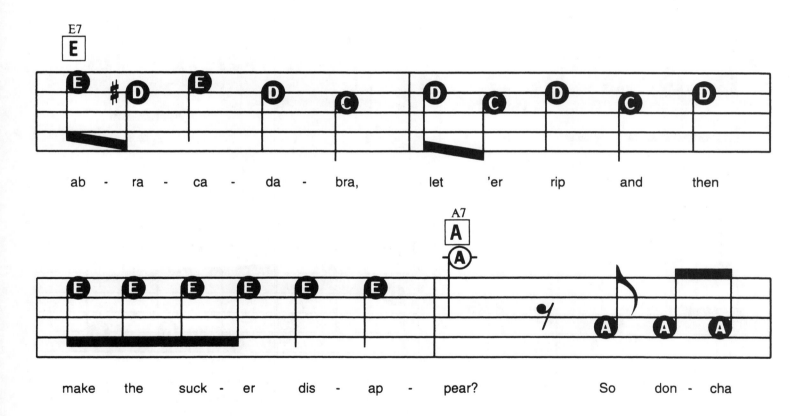

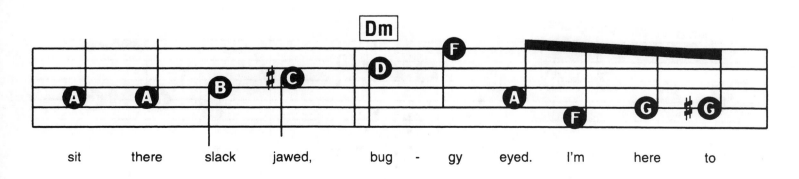

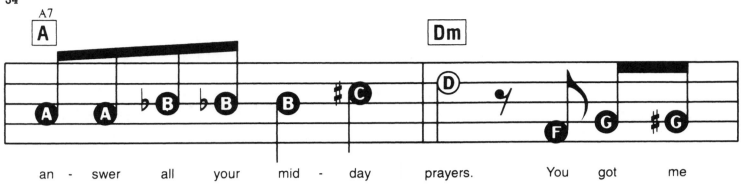

an - swer all your mid - day prayers. You got me

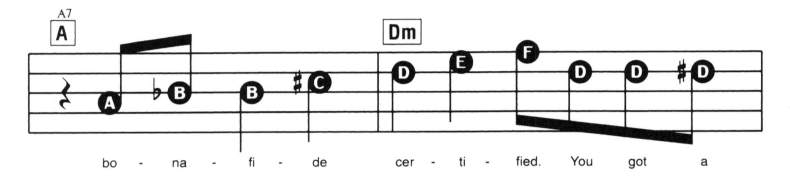

bo - na - fi - de cer - ti - fied. You got a

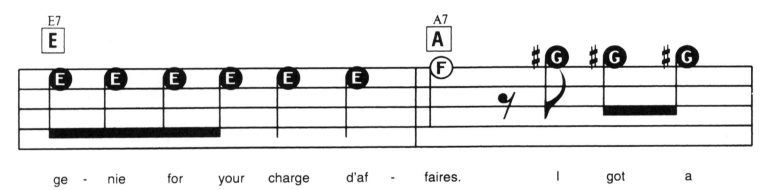

ge - nie for your charge d'af - faires. I got a

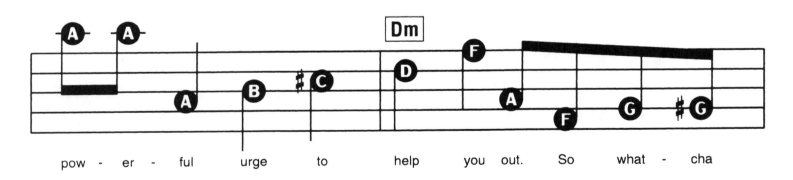

pow - er - ful urge to help you out. So what - cha

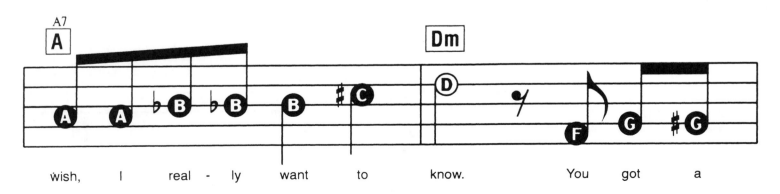

wish, I real - ly want to know. You got a

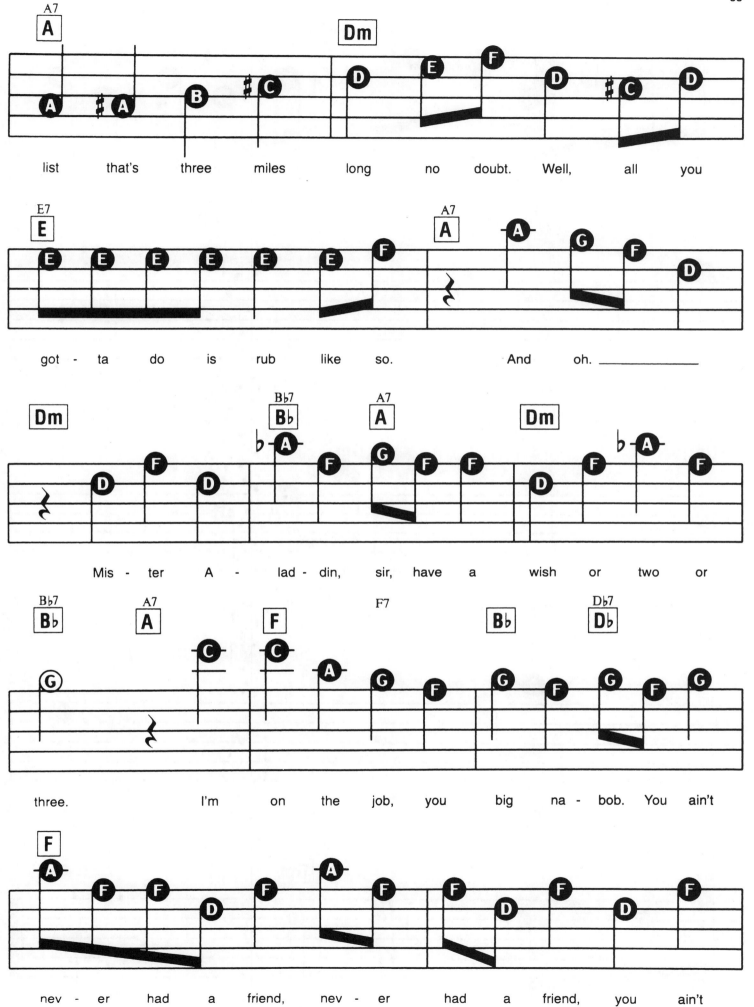

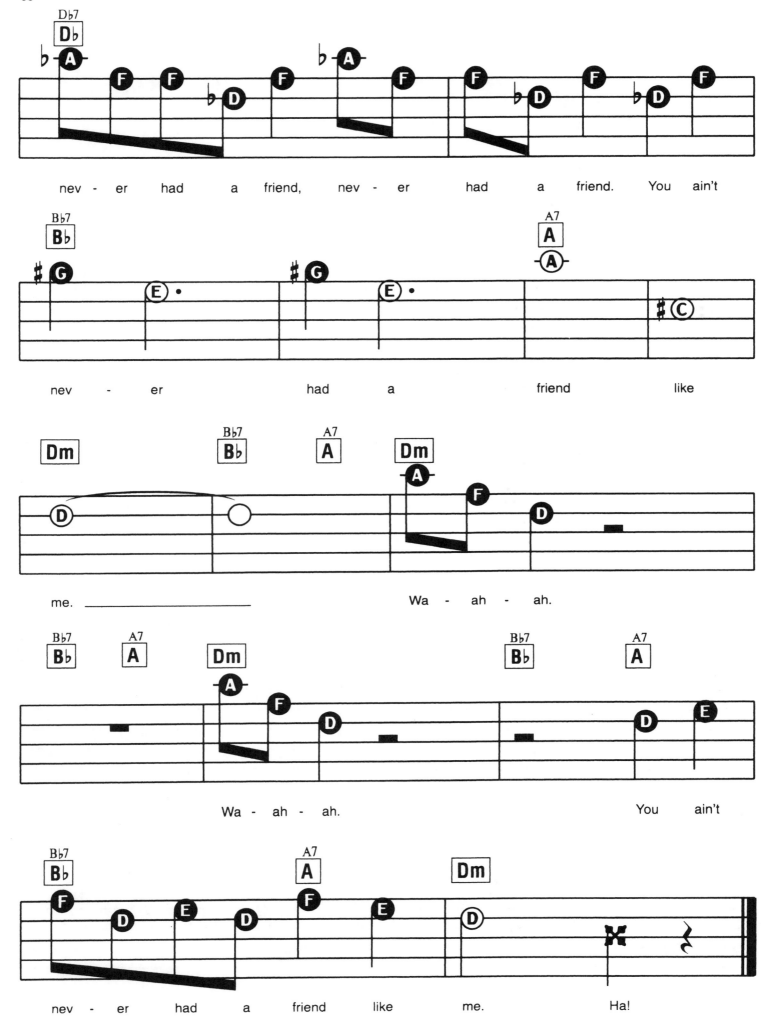

Hakuna Matata
from THE LION KING

Registration 5
Rhythm: Swing

Music by Elton John
Lyrics by Tim Rice

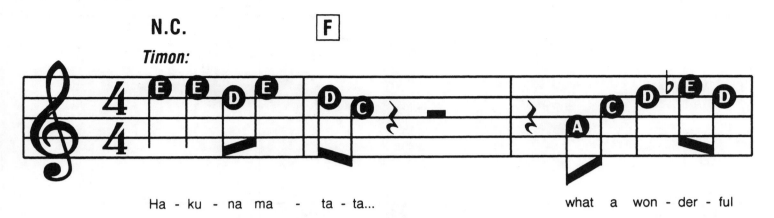

Ha - ku - na ma - ta - ta... what a won - der - ful

phrase! Ha - ku - na ma - ta - ta...

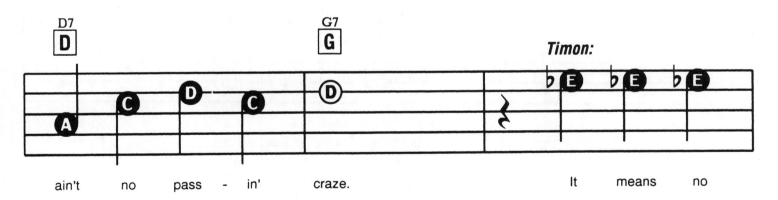

ain't no pass - in' craze. It means no

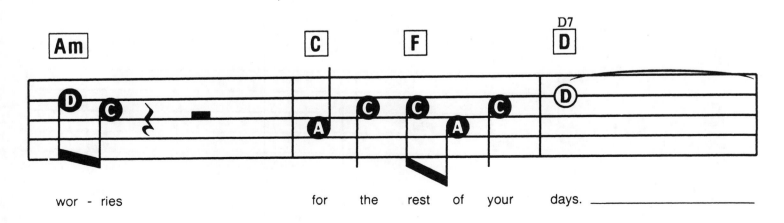

wor - ries for the rest of your days. _____

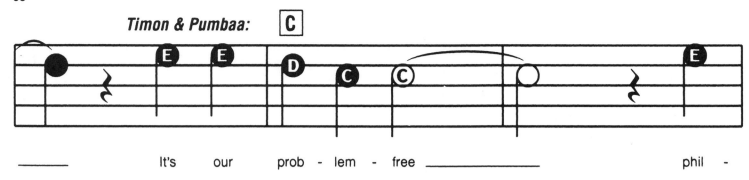

_____ It's our prob - lem - free _____ phil -

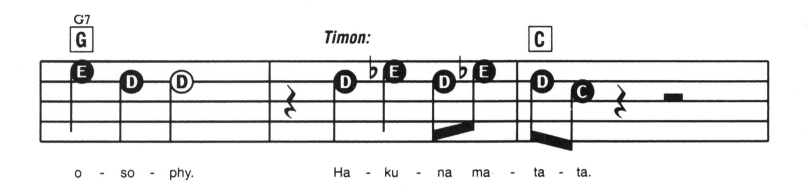

o - so - phy.   Ha - ku - na ma - ta - ta.

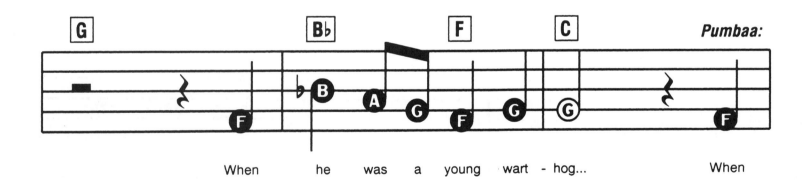

When   he   was   a   young   wart - hog...   When

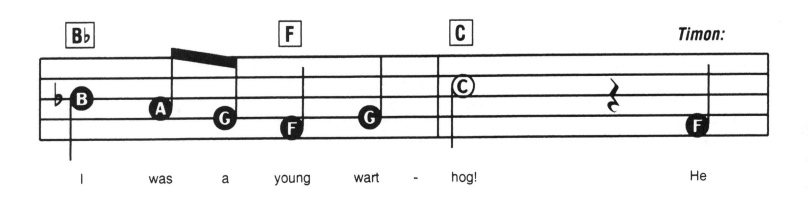

I   was   a   young   wart - hog!   He

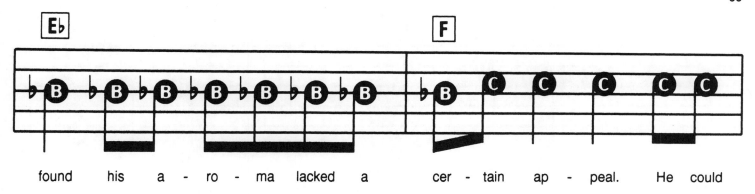

found his a - ro - ma lacked a cer - tain ap - peal. He could

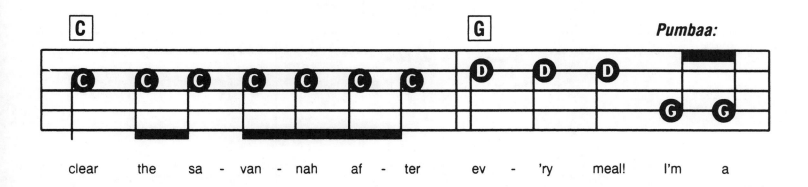

clear the sa - van - nah af - ter ev - 'ry meal! I'm a

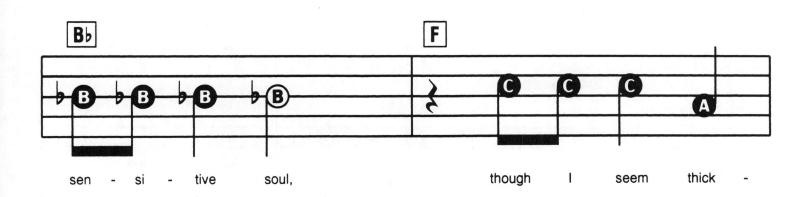

sen - si - tive soul, though I seem thick -

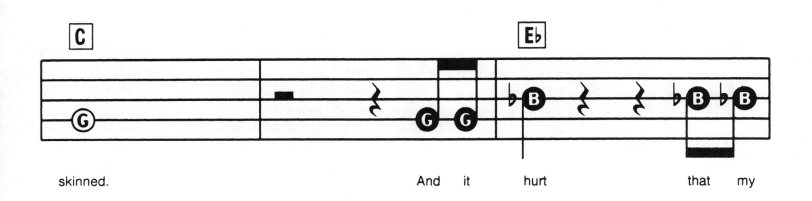

skinned. And it hurt that my

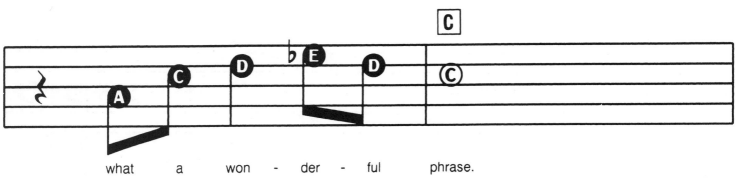

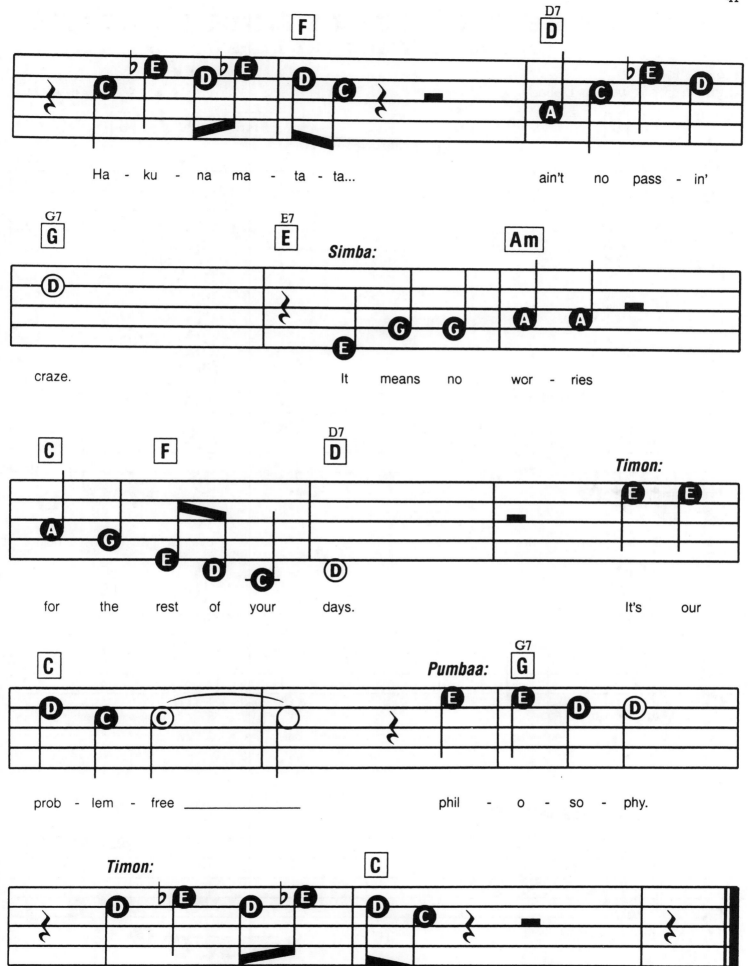

How Does a Moment Last Forever
from BEAUTY AND THE BEAST

Registration 1
Rhythm: Broadway or Ballad

Music by Alan Menken
Lyrics by Tim Rice

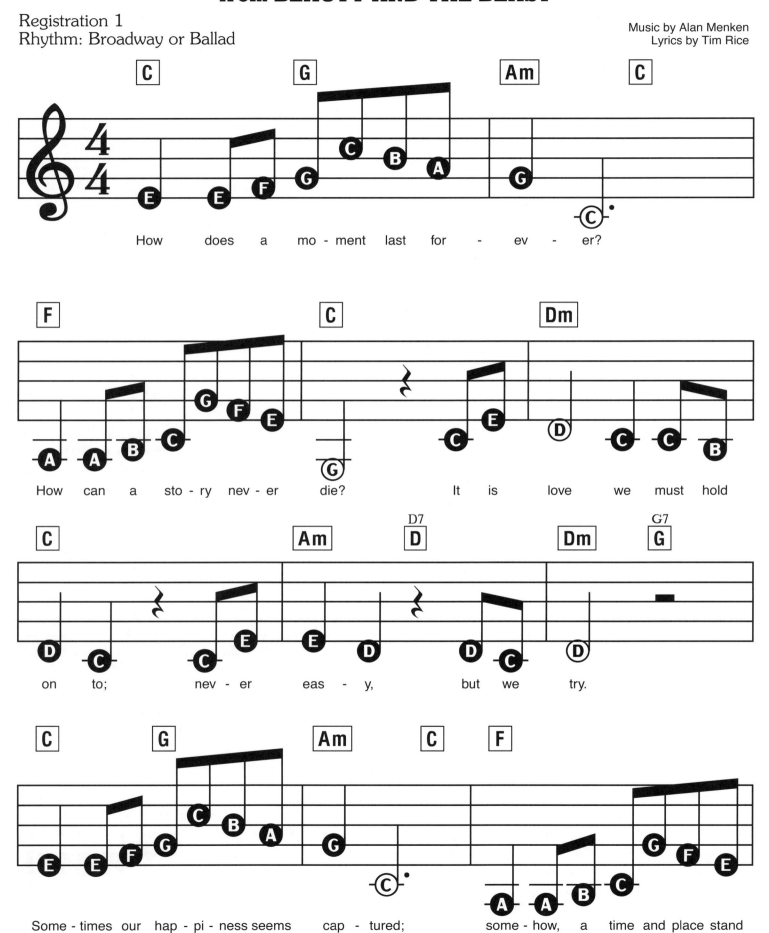

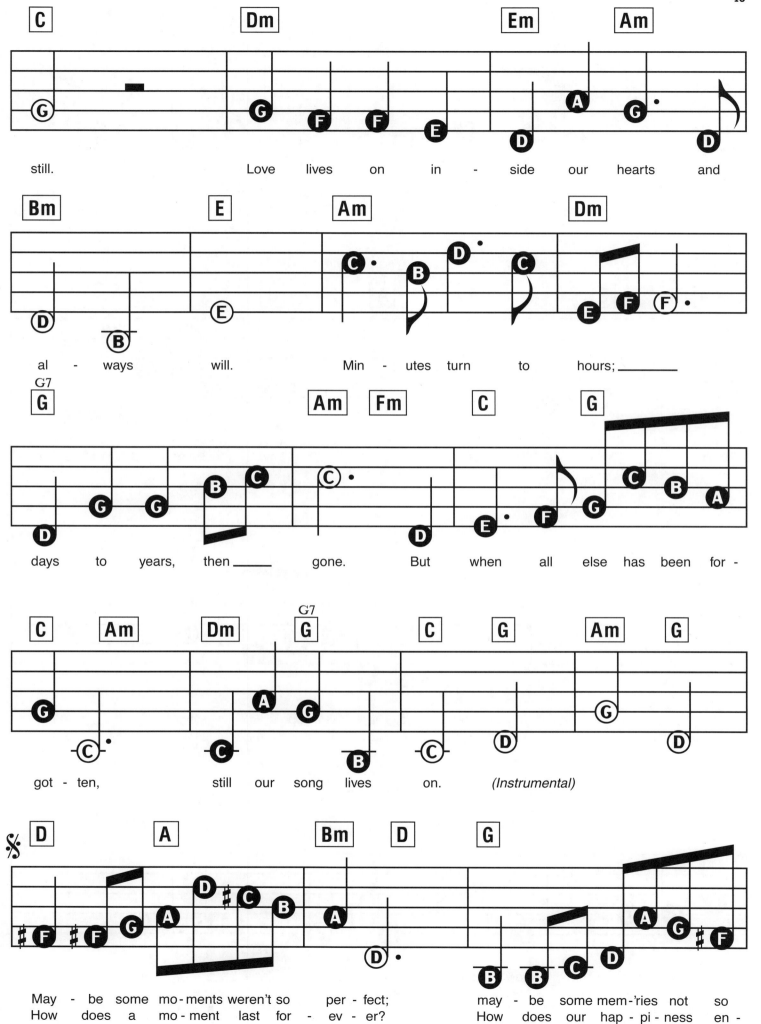

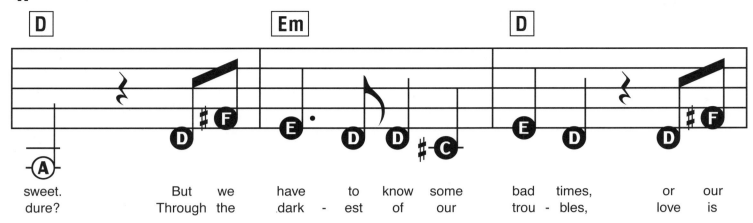

sweet. But we have to know some bad times, or our
dure? Through the dark - est of our trou - bles, love is

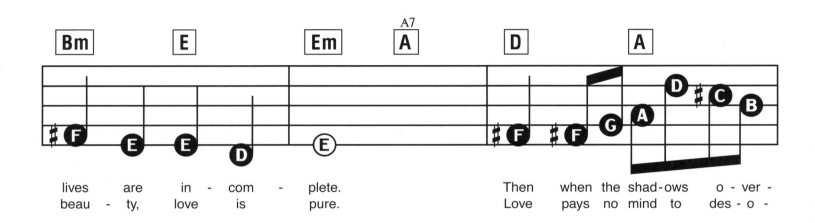

lives are in - com - plete. Then when the shad-ows o - ver-
beau - ty, love is pure. Love pays no mind to des - o -

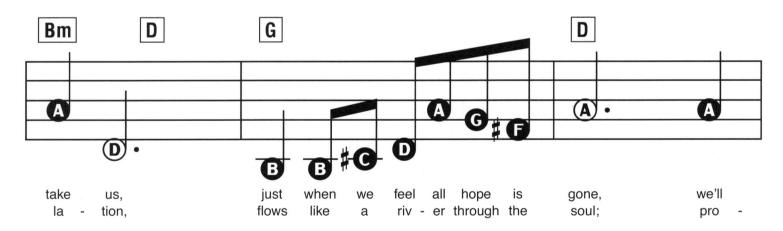

take us, just when we feel all hope is gone, we'll
la - tion, flows like a riv - er through the soul; pro -

To Coda

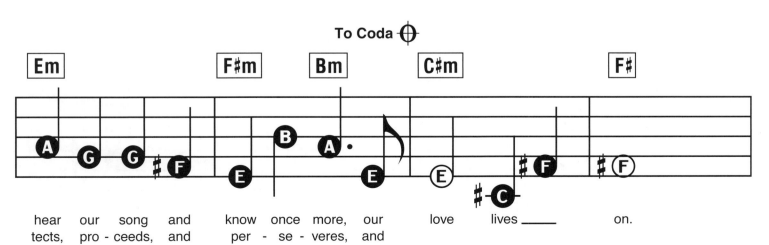

hear our song and know once more, our love lives _____ on.
tects, pro - ceeds, and per - se - veres, and

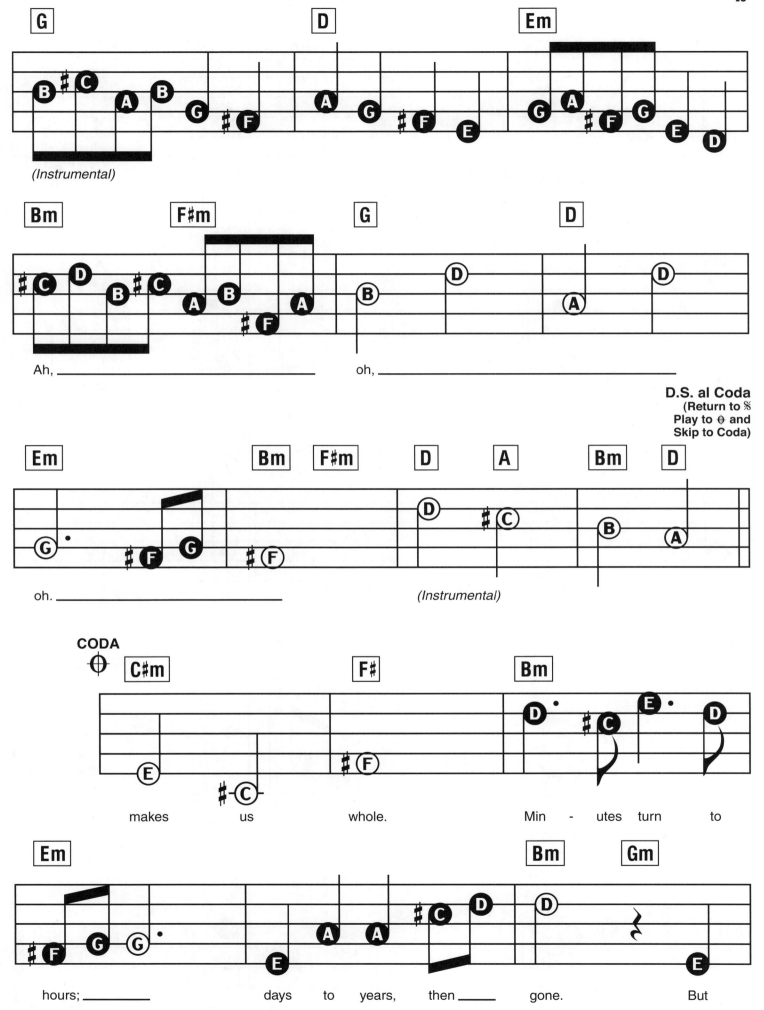

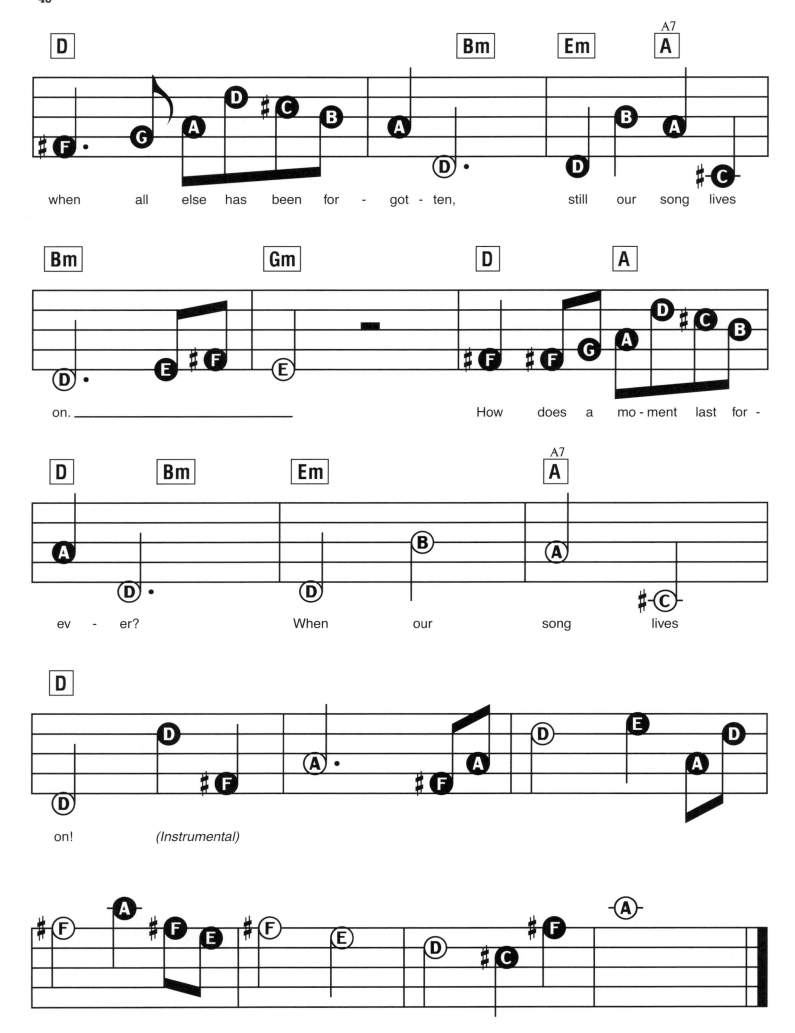

How Far I'll Go
from MOANA

Registration 1
Rhythm: Pop or Techno

Music and Lyrics by
Lin-Manuel Miranda

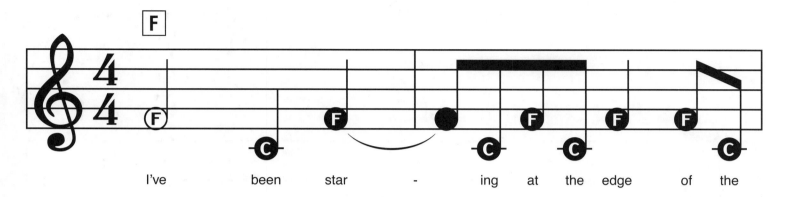

I've been star - ing at the edge of the

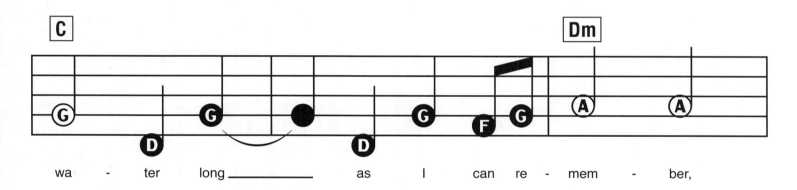

wa - ter long _____ as I can re - mem - ber,

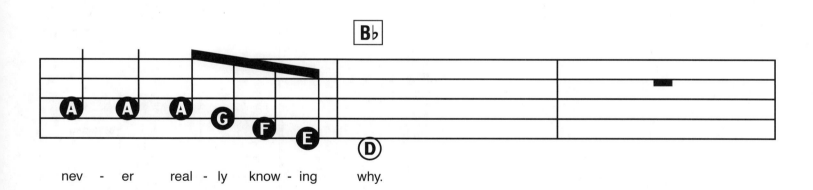

nev - er real - ly know - ing why.

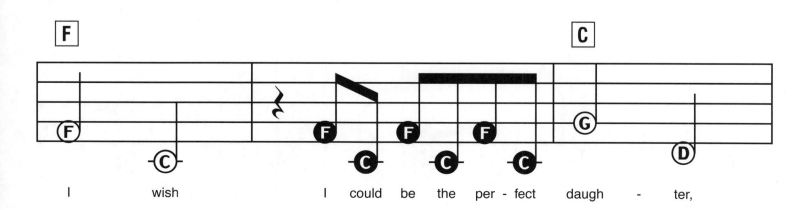

I wish I could be the per - fect daugh - ter,

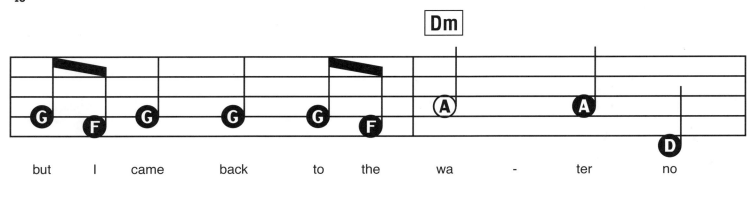

but I came back to the wa - ter no

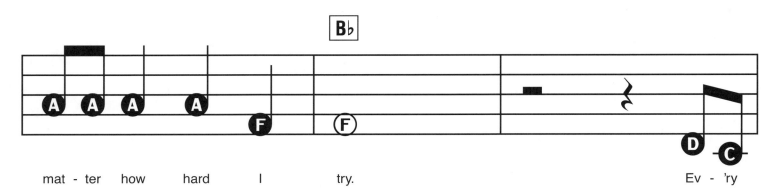

mat - ter how hard I try. Ev - 'ry

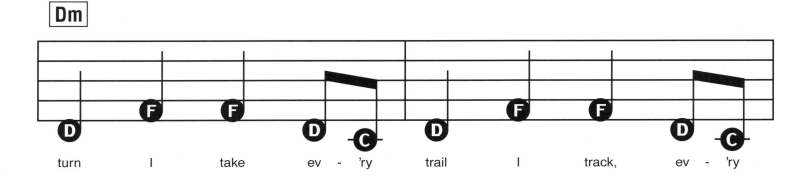

turn I take ev - 'ry trail I track, ev - 'ry

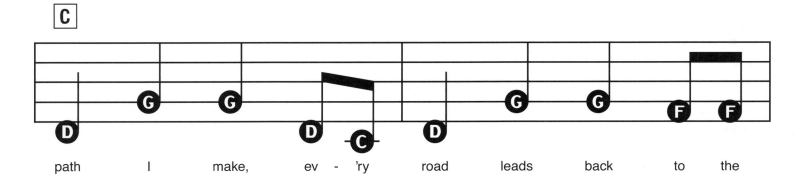

path I make, ev - 'ry road leads back to the

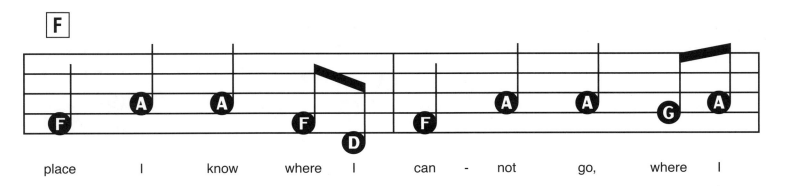

place I know where I can - not go, where I

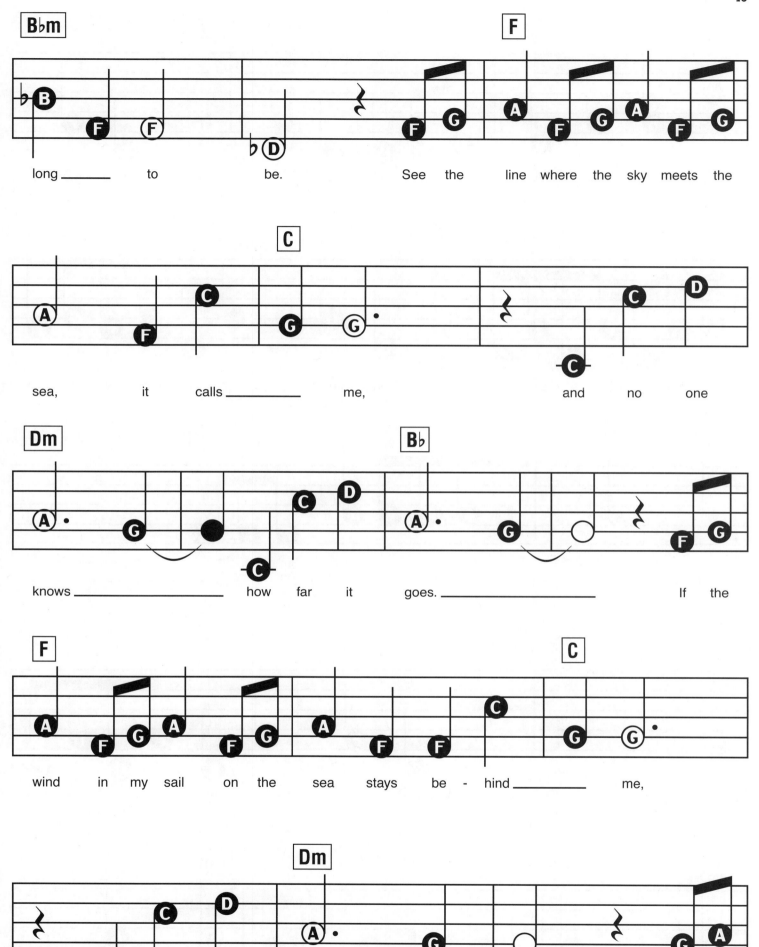

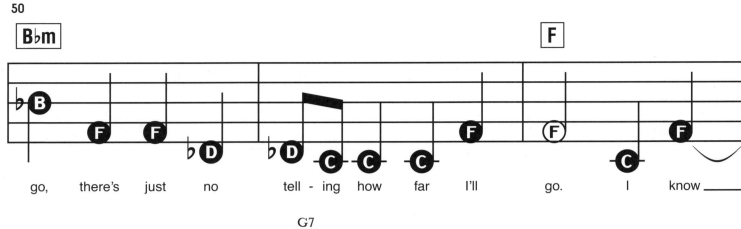

go, there's just no tell-ing how far I'll go. I know ____

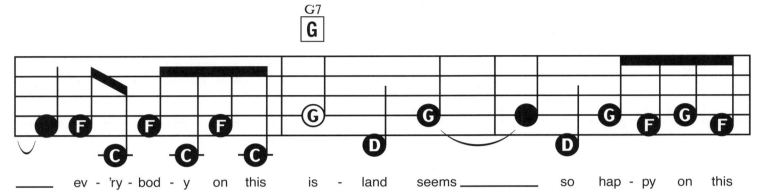

____ ev-'ry-bod-y on this is-land seems ____ so hap-py on this

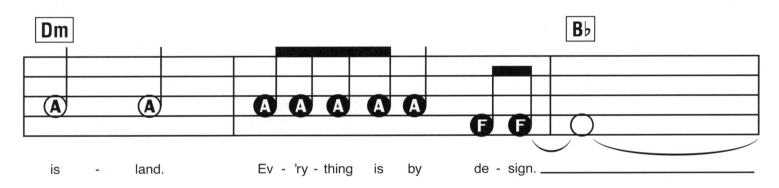

is-land. Ev-'ry-thing is by de-sign. ____

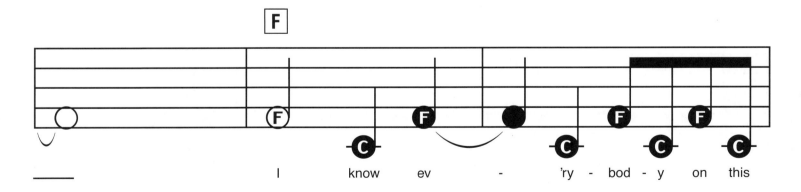

____ I know ev - 'ry-bod-y on this

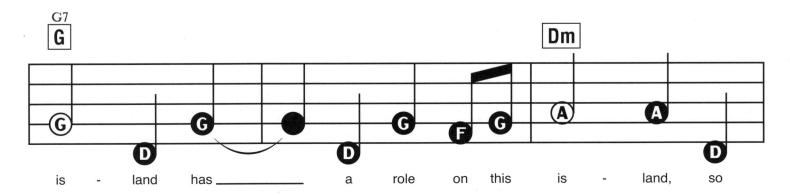

is-land has ____ a role on this is-land, so

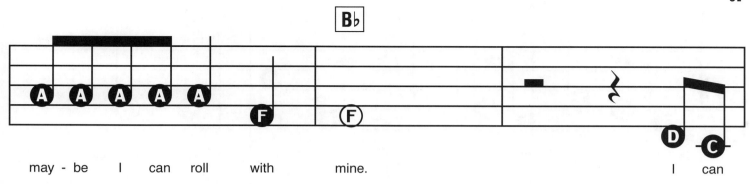

may - be I can roll with mine.   I can

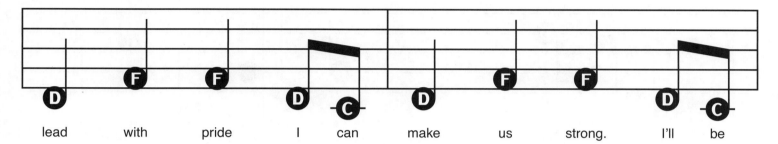

lead with pride I can make us strong. I'll be

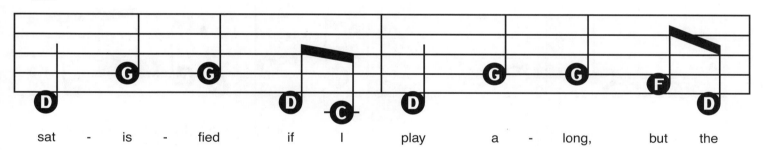

sat - is - fied if I play a - long, but the

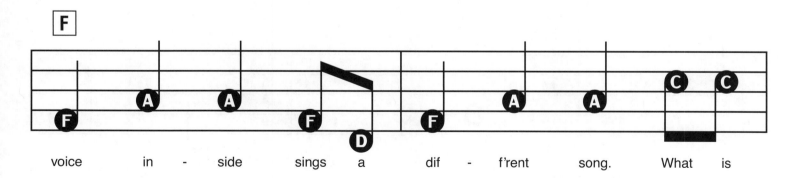

voice in - side sings a dif - f'rent song. What is

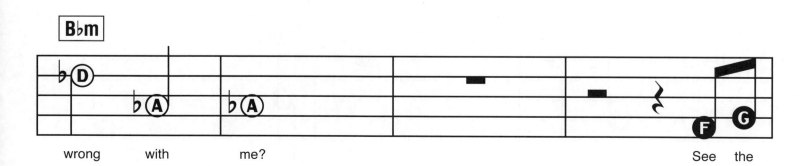

wrong with me?   See the

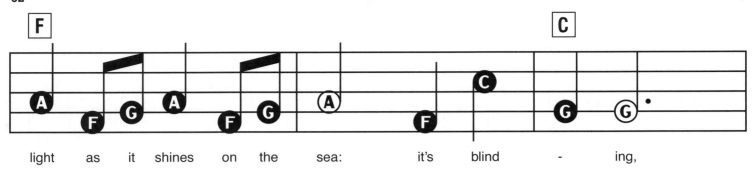

light as it shines on the sea: it's blind - ing,

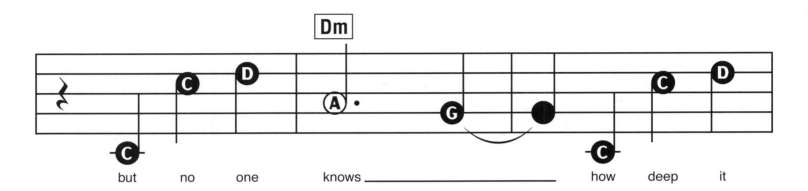

but no one knows _____ how deep it

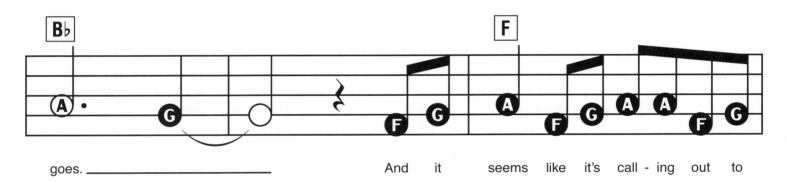

goes. _____ And it seems like it's call - ing out to

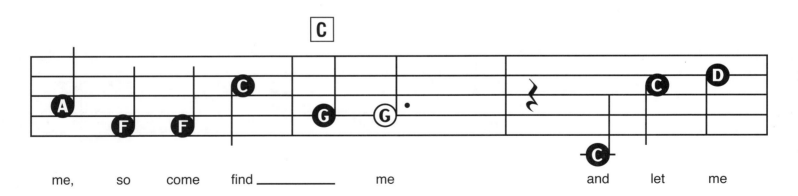

me, so come find _____ me and let me

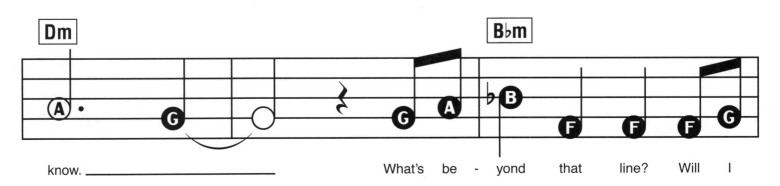

know. _____ What's be - yond that line? Will I

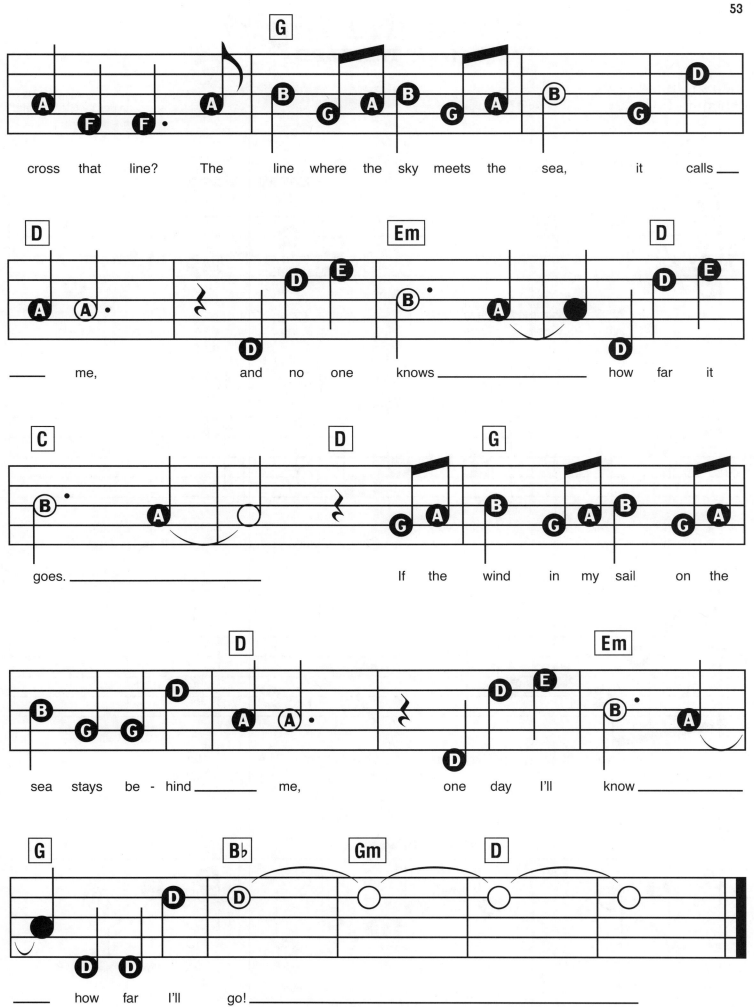

I See the Light
from TANGLED

Registration 4
Rhythm: Folk

Music by Alan Menken
Lyrics by Glenn Slater

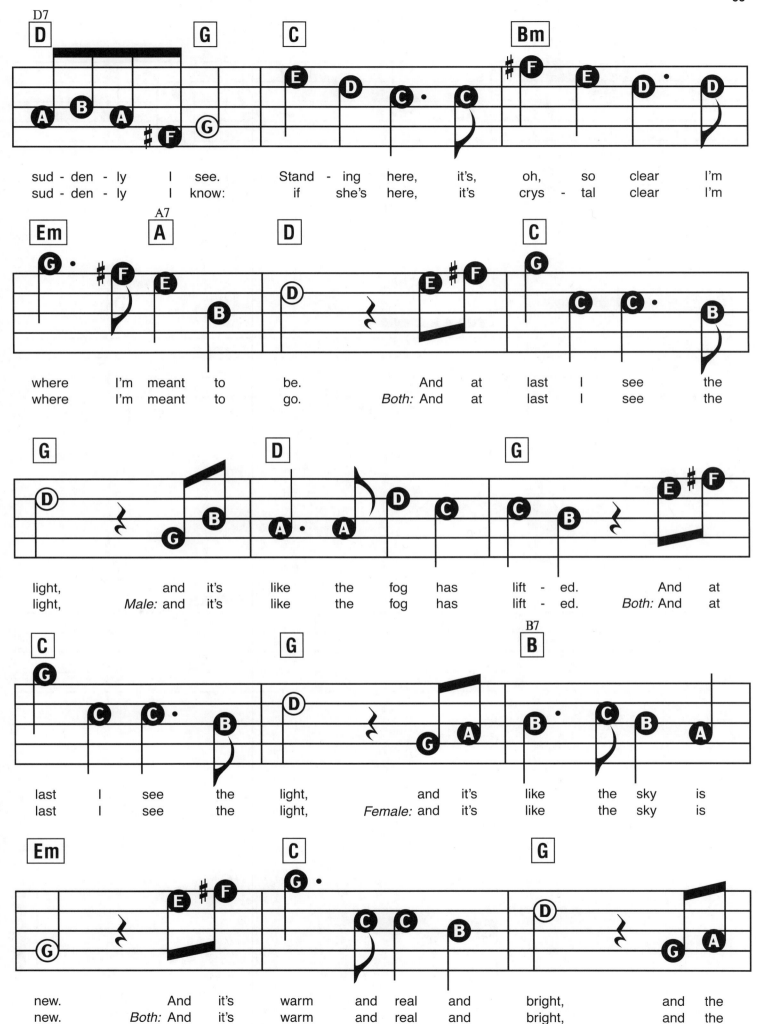

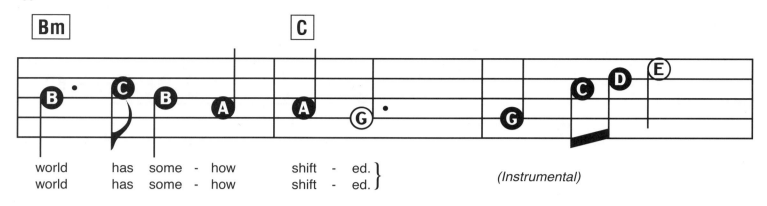

world has some - how shift - ed.
world has some - how shift - ed. } *(Instrumental)*

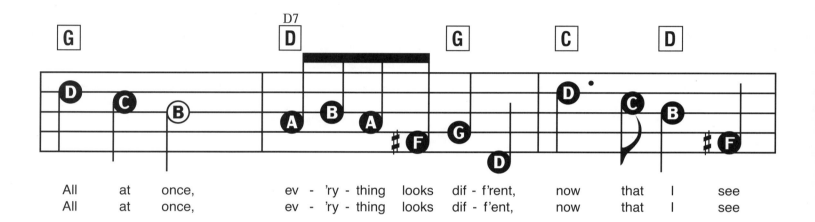

All at once, ev - 'ry - thing looks dif - f'rent, now that I see
All at once, ev - 'ry - thing looks dif - f'ent, now that I see

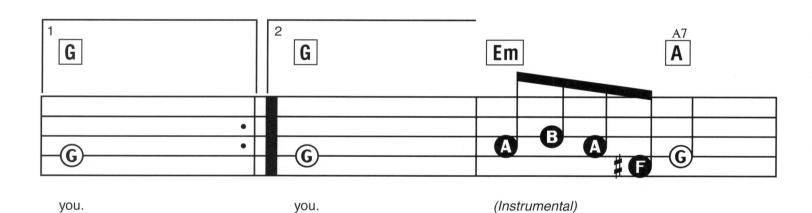

you.
you.

(Instrumental)

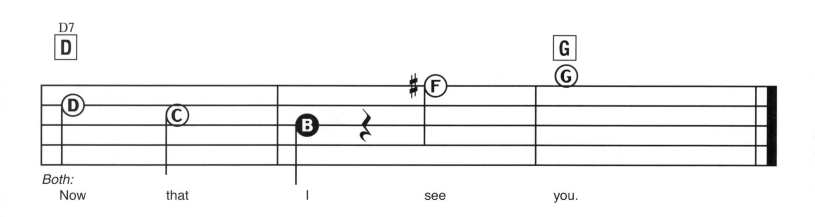

Both:
Now that I see you.

Let It Go
from FROZEN

Registration 8
Rhythm: Rock or Dance

Music and Lyrics by Kristen Anderson-Lopez
and Robert Lopez

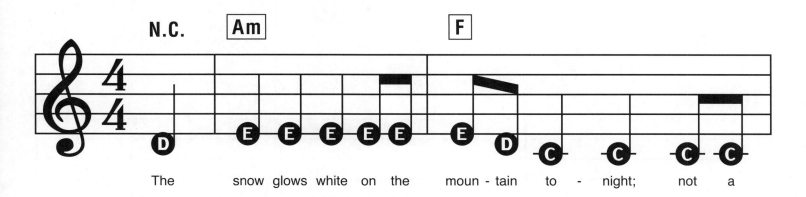

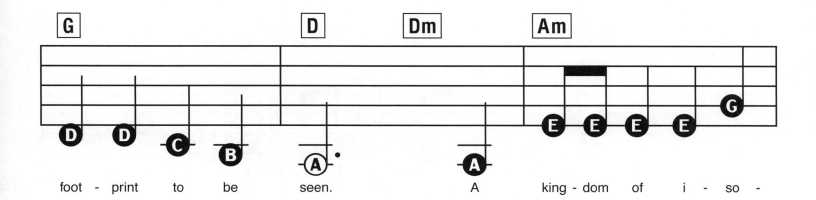

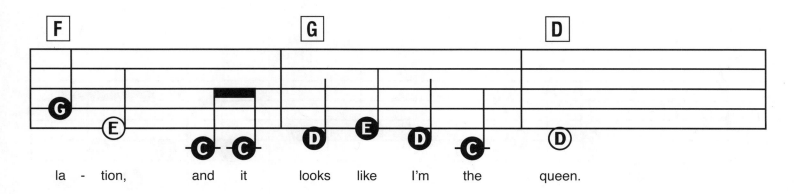

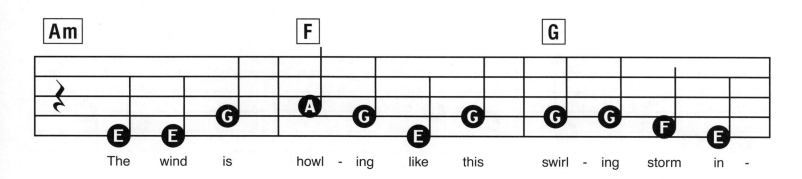

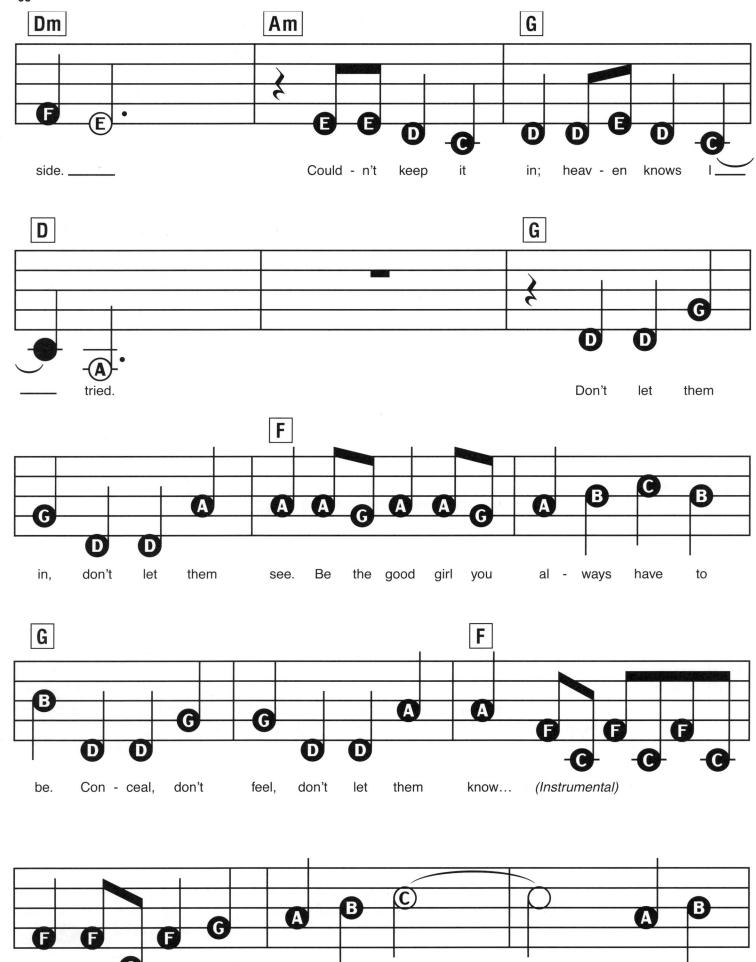

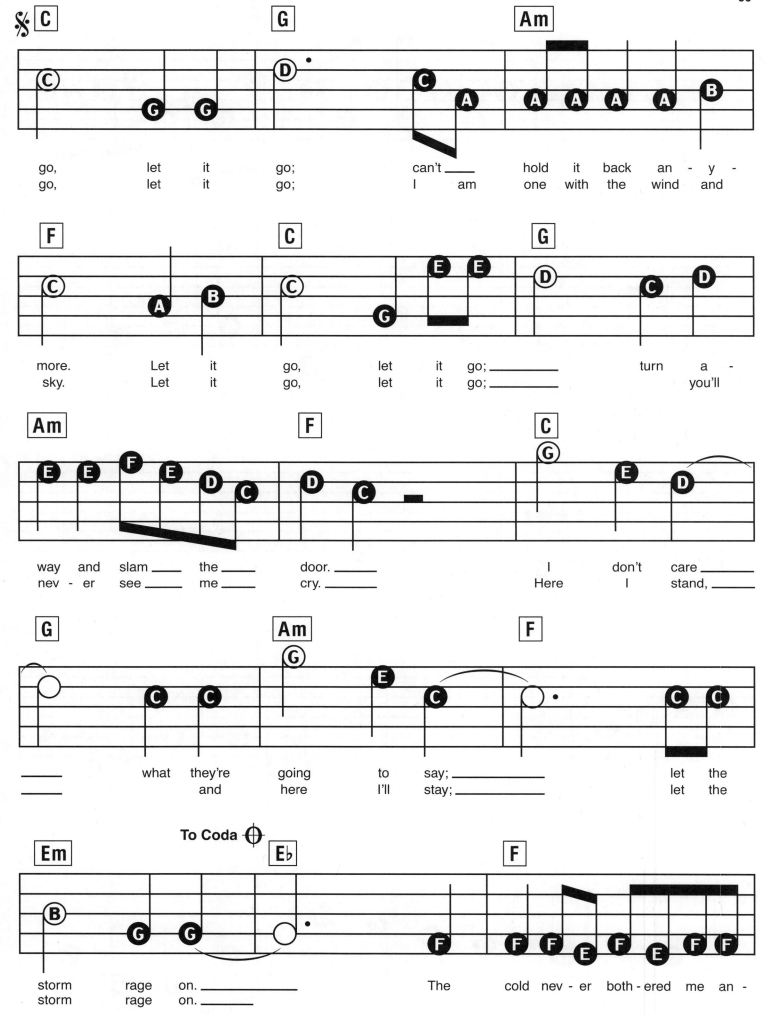

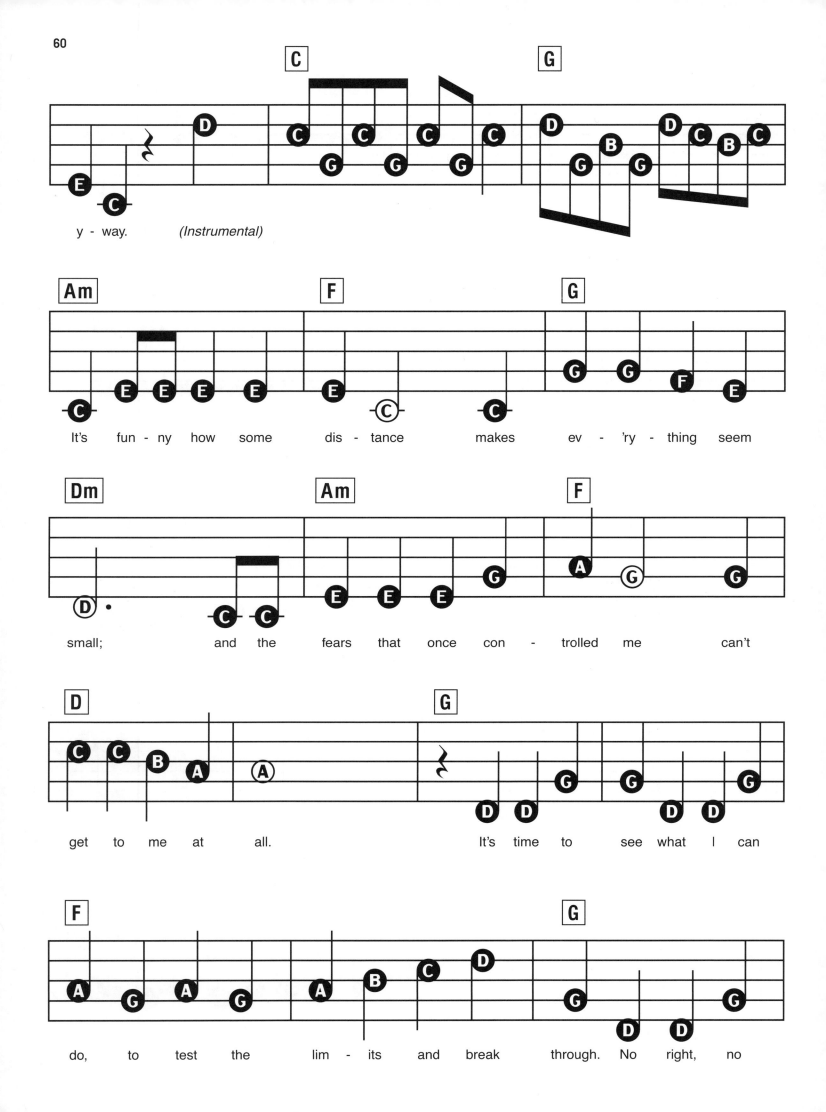

D.S. al Coda
(Return to ℅
Play to ⊕ and
Skip to Coda)

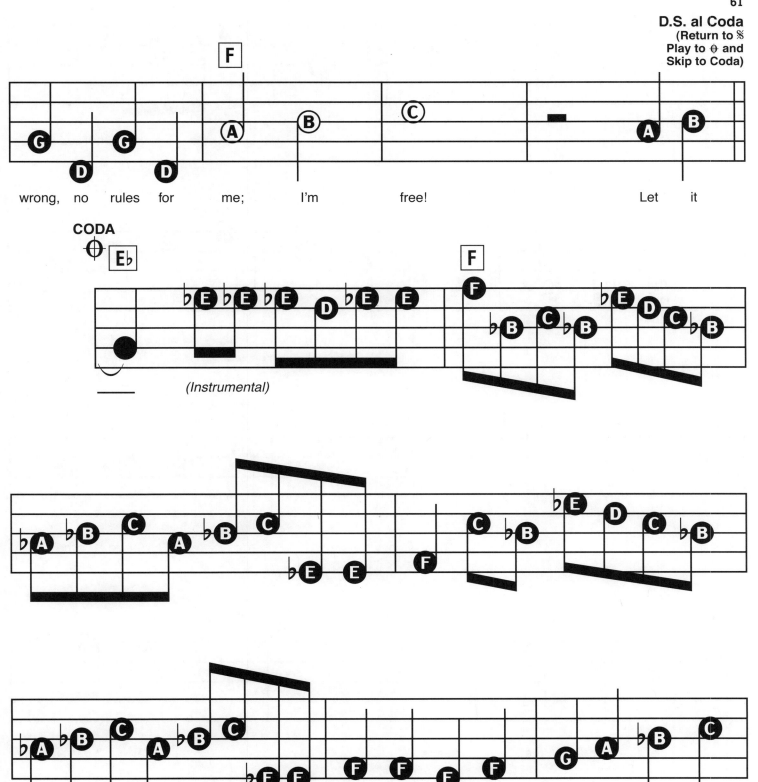

wrong, no rules for me; I'm free! Let it

CODA

Eb

(Instrumental)

My pow - er flur - ries through the

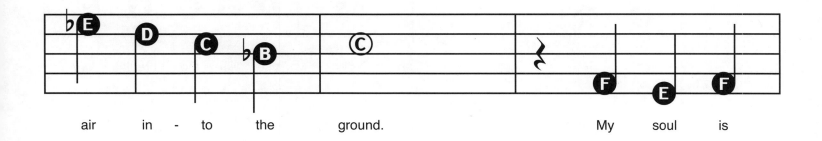

air in - to the ground. My soul is

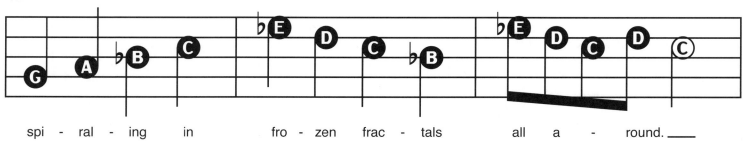

spi - ral - ing in fro - zen frac - tals all a - round. ____

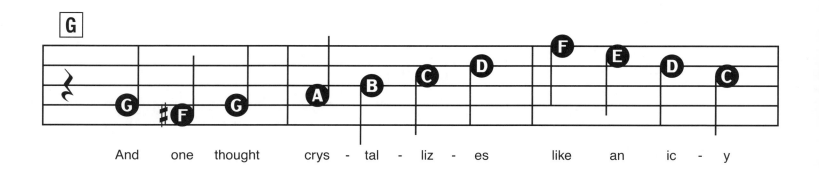

And one thought crys - tal - liz - es like an ic - y

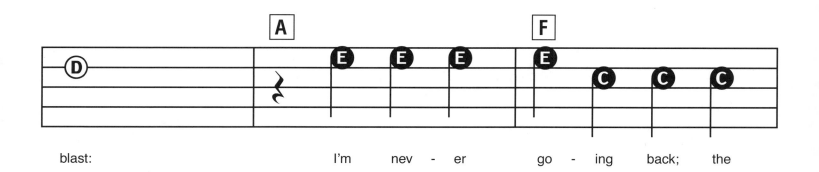

blast: I'm nev - er go - ing back; the

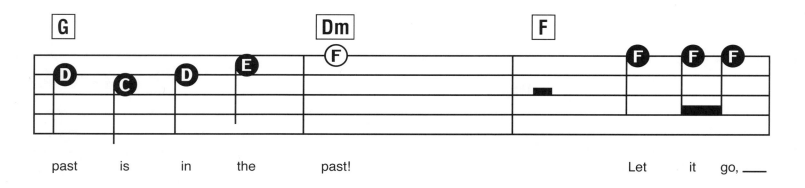

past is in the past! Let it go, ____

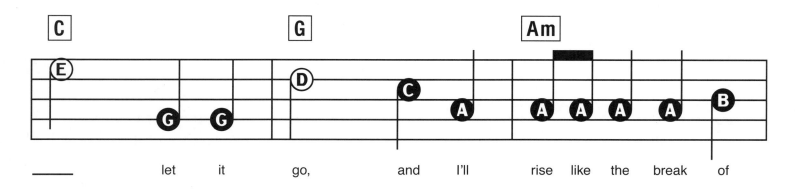

____ let it go, and I'll rise like the break of

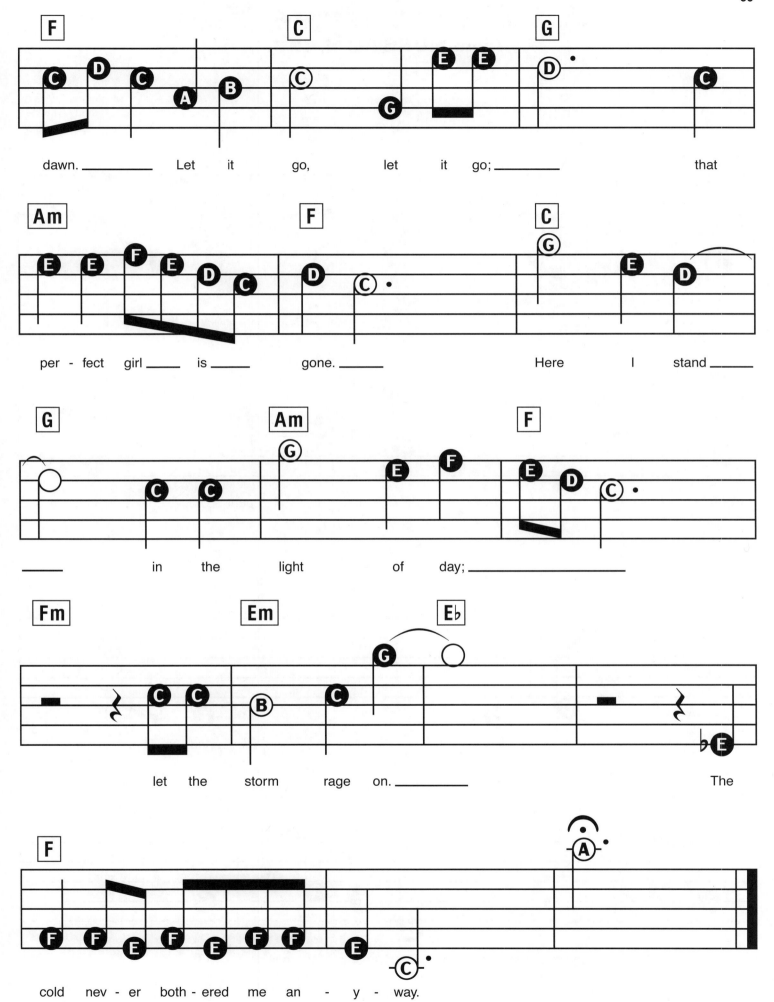

If I Didn't Have You
from MONSTERS, INC.

Registration 7
Rhythm: Fox Trot or Swing

Music and Lyrics by
Randy Newman

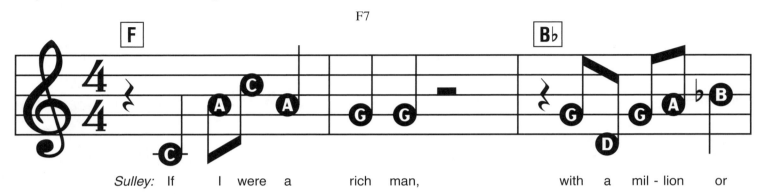

Sulley: If I were a rich man, with a mil - lion or

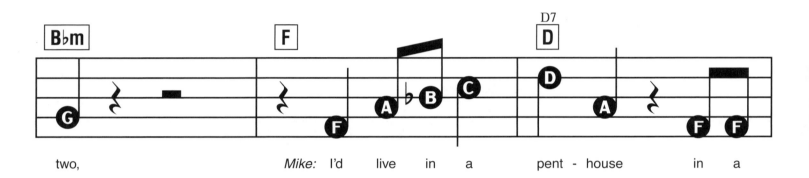

two, *Mike:* I'd live in a pent - house in a

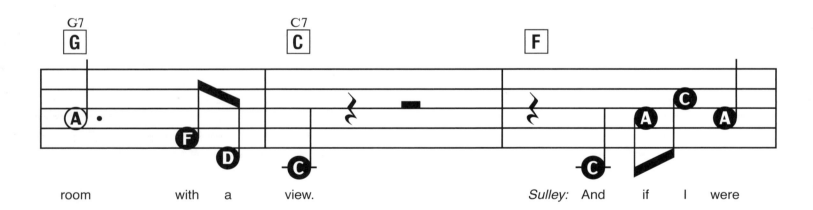

room with a view. *Sulley:* And if I were

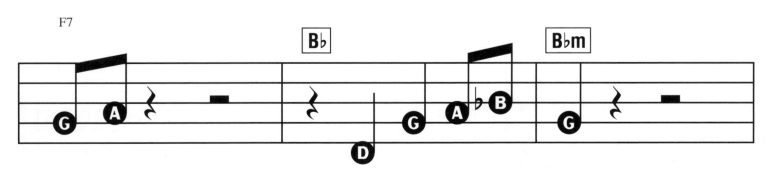

hand - some, (It could happen,) *Sulley:* 'cause dreams do come true,
(Spoken:) *Mike:* No way!

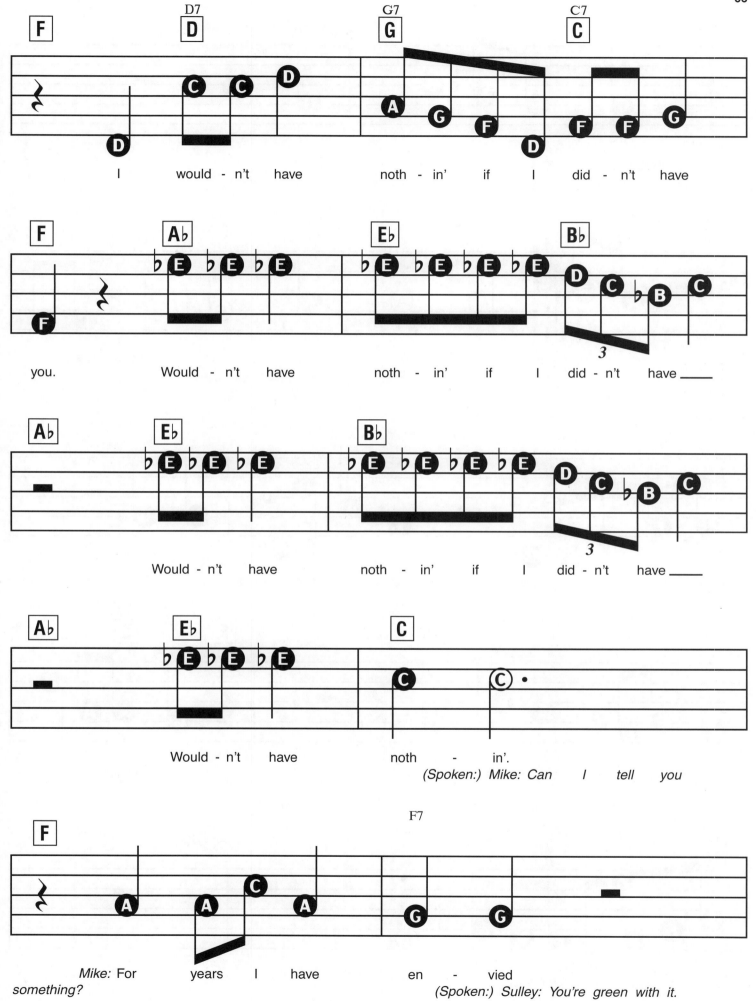

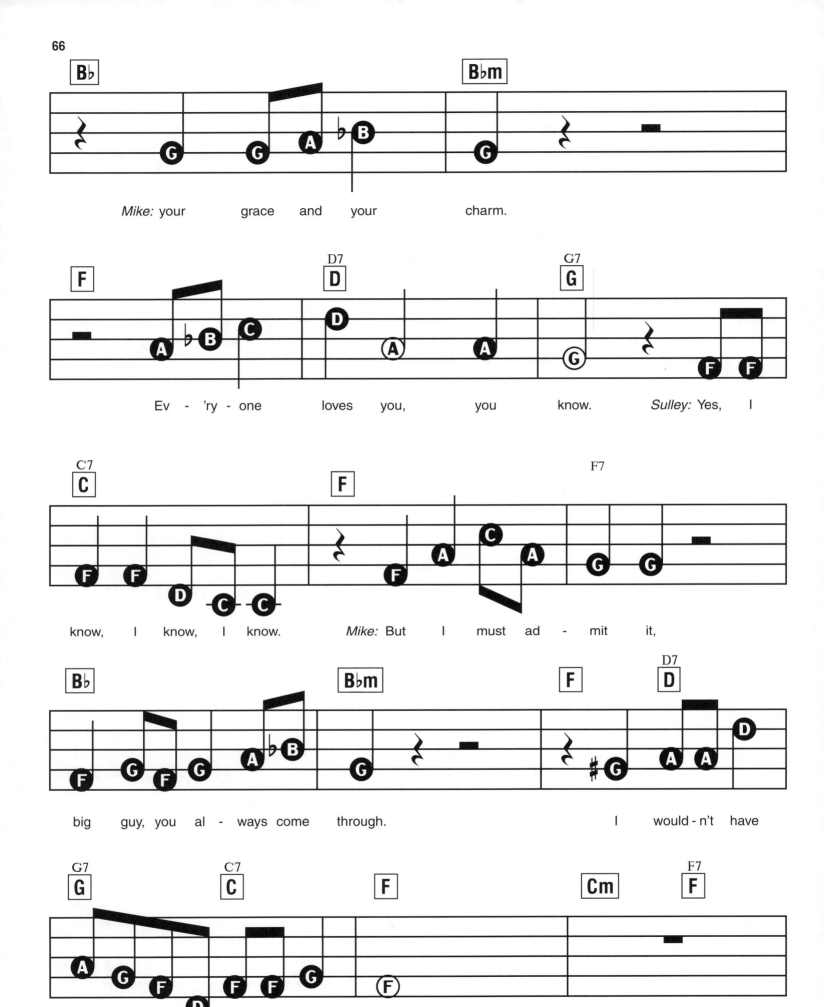

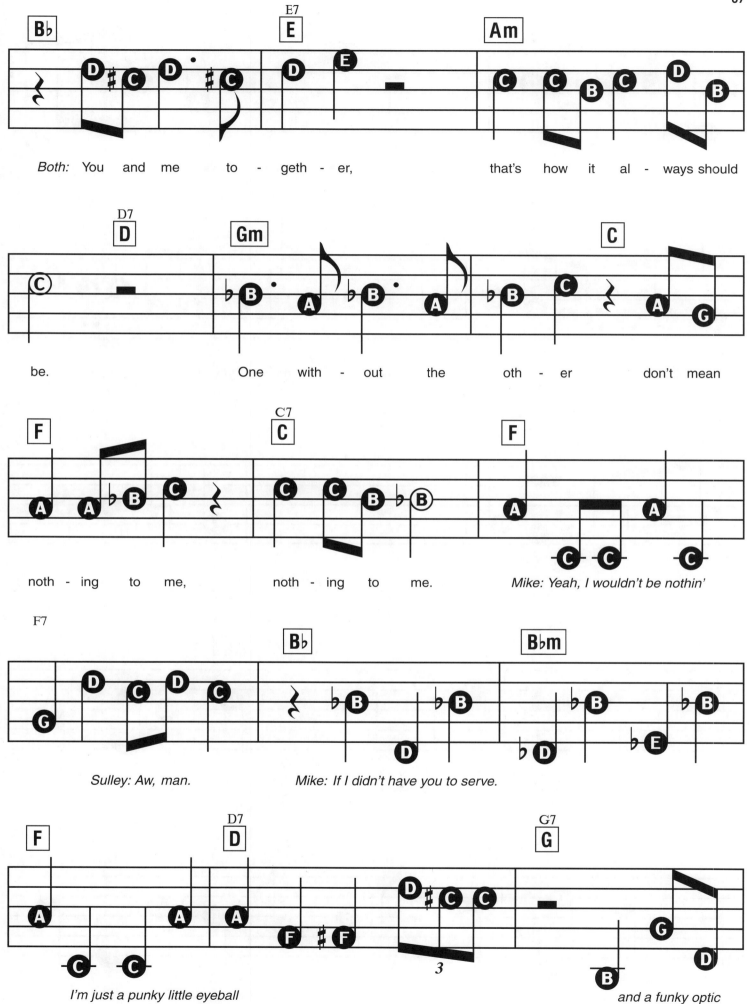

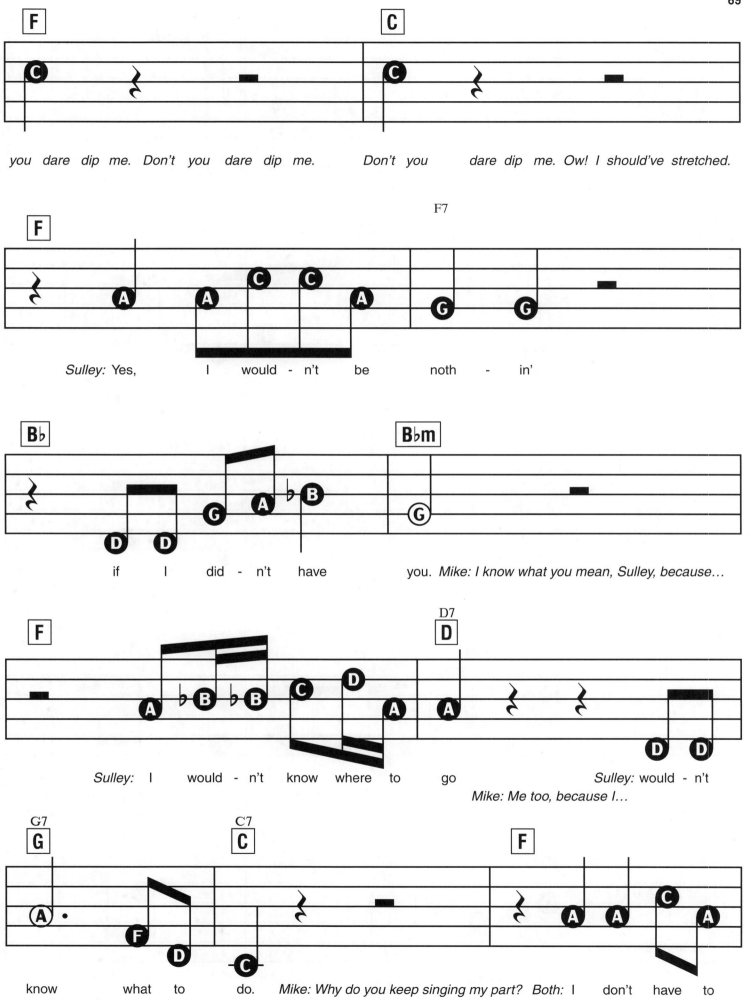

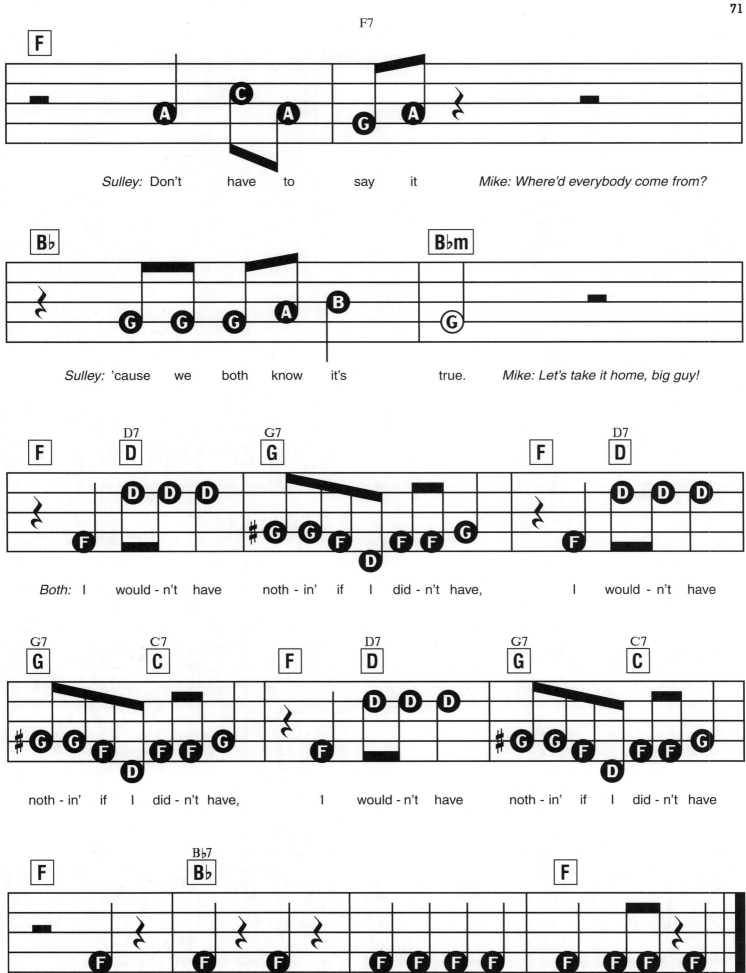

Lava
from LAVA

Registration 4
Rhythm: Folk or Swing

Music and Lyrics by
James Ford Murphy

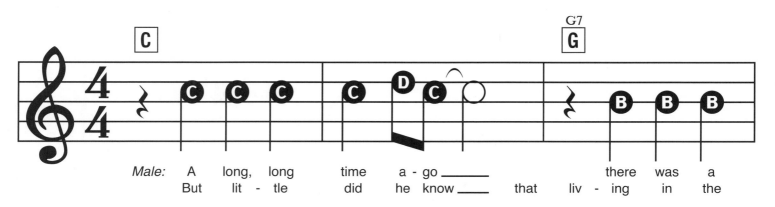

Male: A long, long time a - go _____ there was a
But lit - tle did he know _____ that liv - ing in the

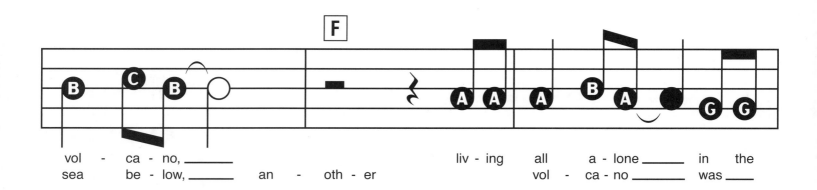

vol - ca - no, _____ liv - ing all a - lone _____ in the
sea be - low, _____ an - oth - er vol - ca - no _____ was

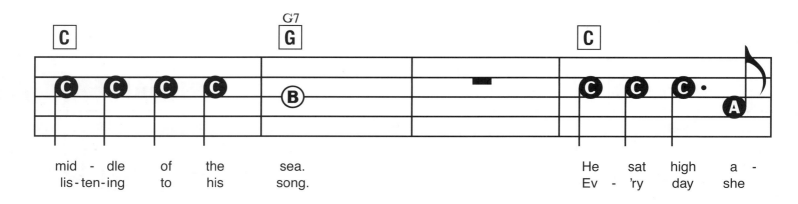

mid - dle of the sea. He sat high a -
lis - ten - ing to his song. Ev - 'ry day she

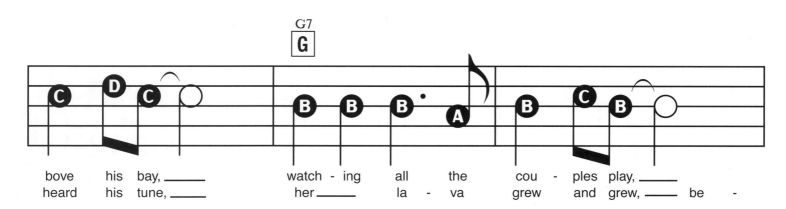

bove his bay, _____ watch - ing all the cou - ples play, _____
heard his tune, _____ her la - va grew and grew, _____ be -

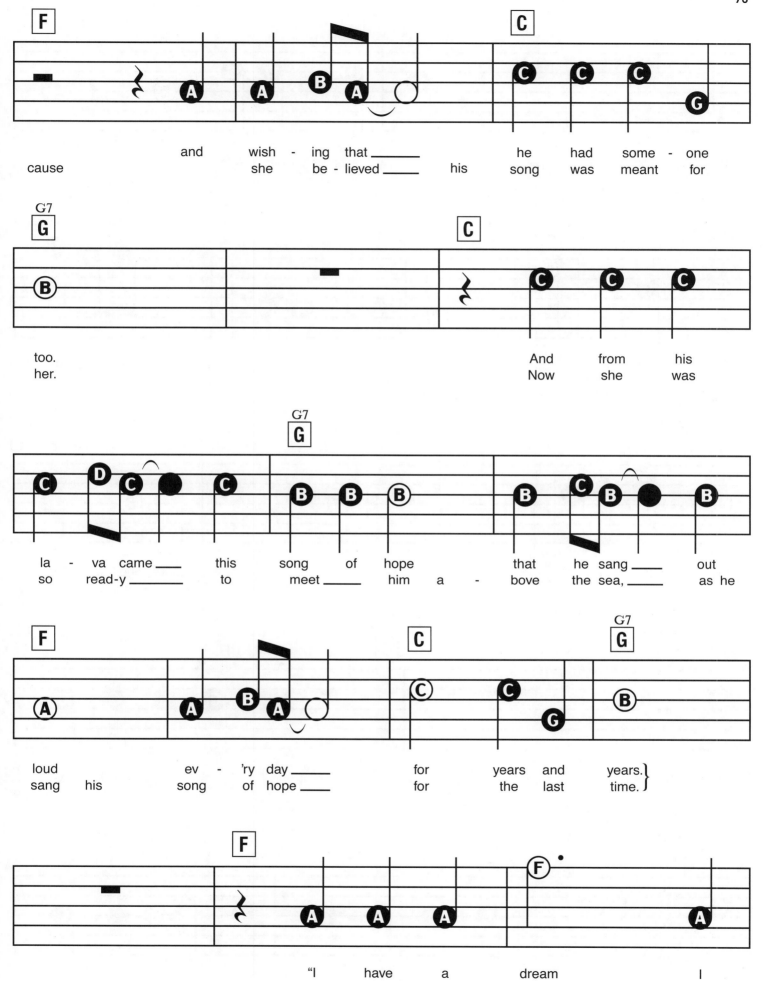

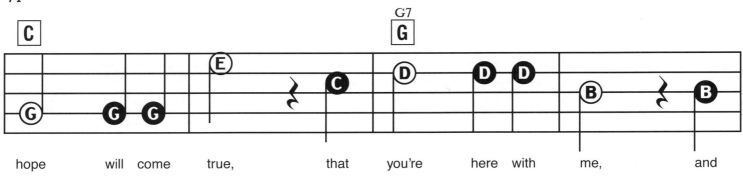

hope   will   come   true,   that   you're   here   with   me,   and

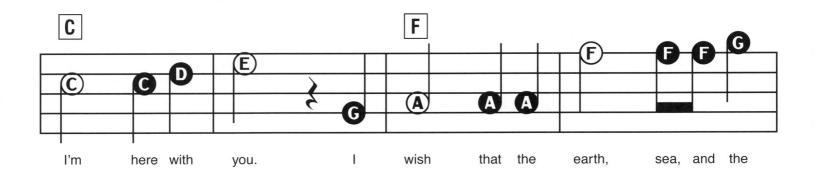

I'm   here   with   you.   I   wish   that   the   earth,   sea,   and   the

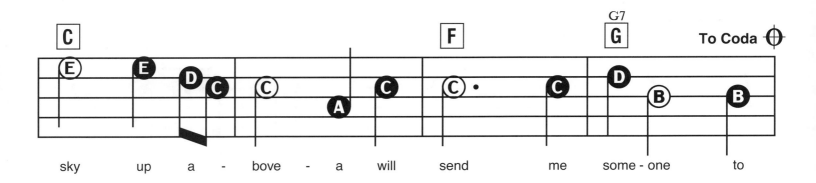

sky   up   a -   bove - a   will   send   me   some - one   to

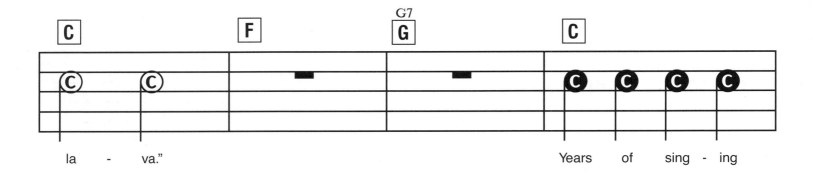

la -   va."   Years   of   sing - ing

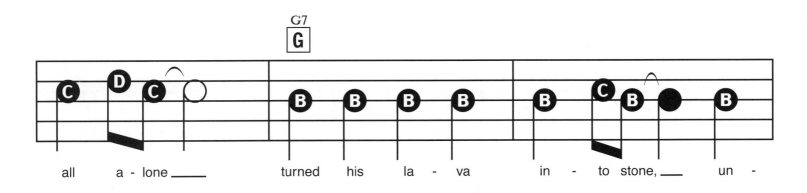

all   a -   lone ____   turned   his   la -   va   in -   to   stone, ___   un -

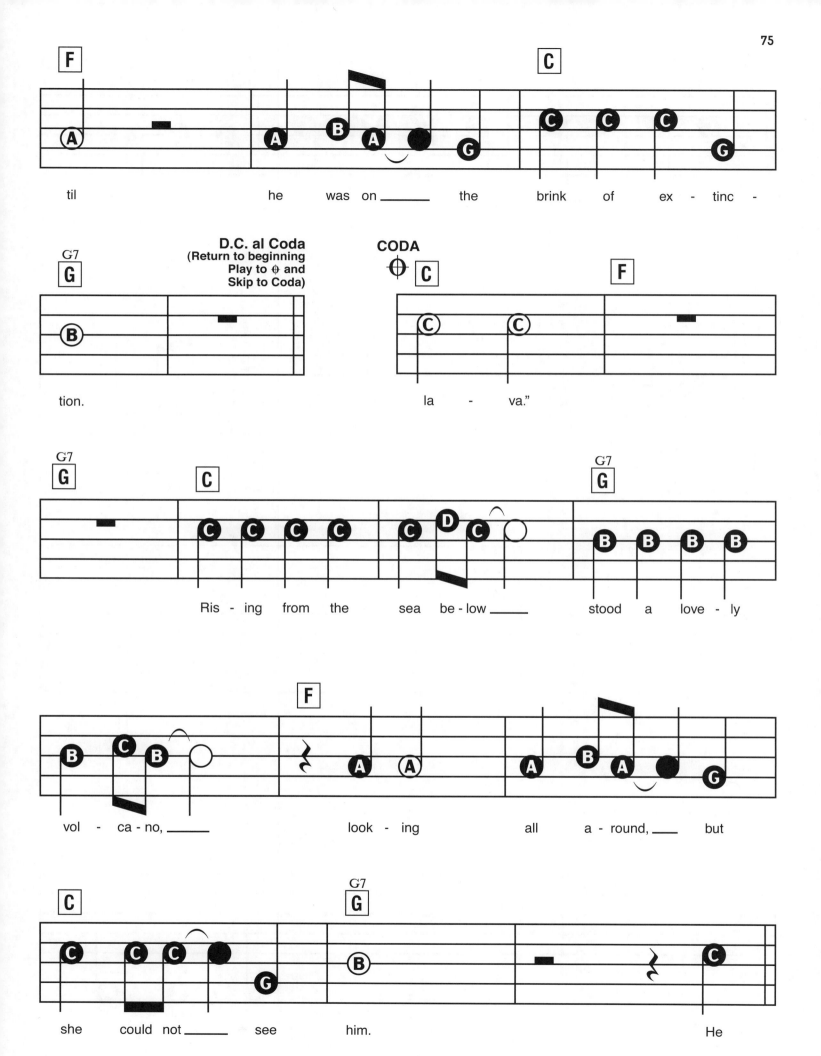

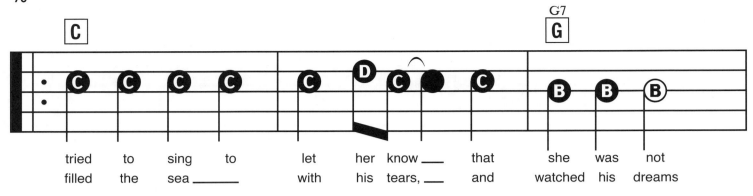

tried to sing to   let her know ___ that   she was not
filled the sea ___ with his tears, ___ and   watched his dreams

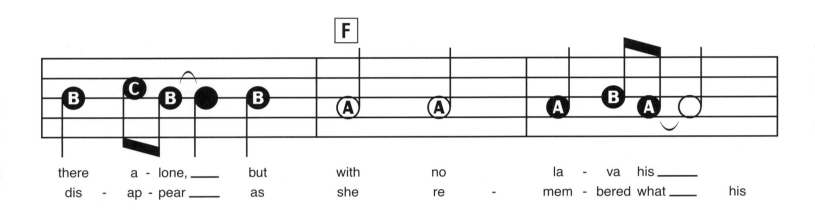

there a - lone, ___ but   with no   la - va his ___
dis - ap - pear ___ as   she re - mem - bered what ___ his

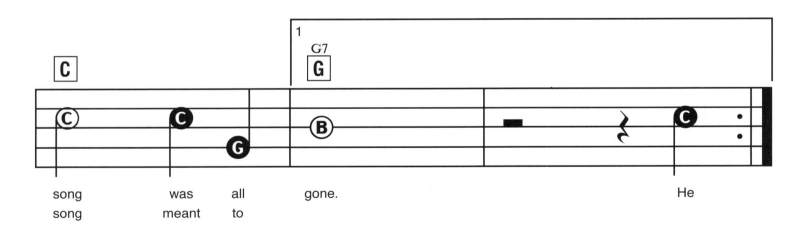

song was all   gone.   He
song meant to

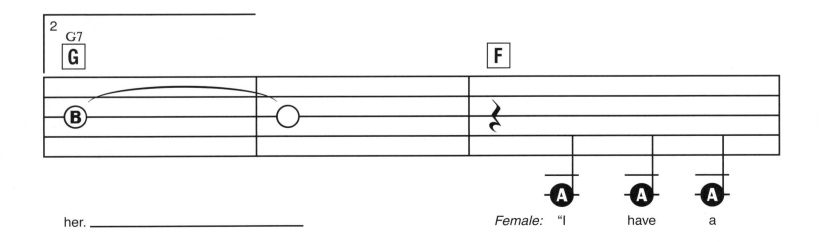

her. ___   *Female:* "I have a

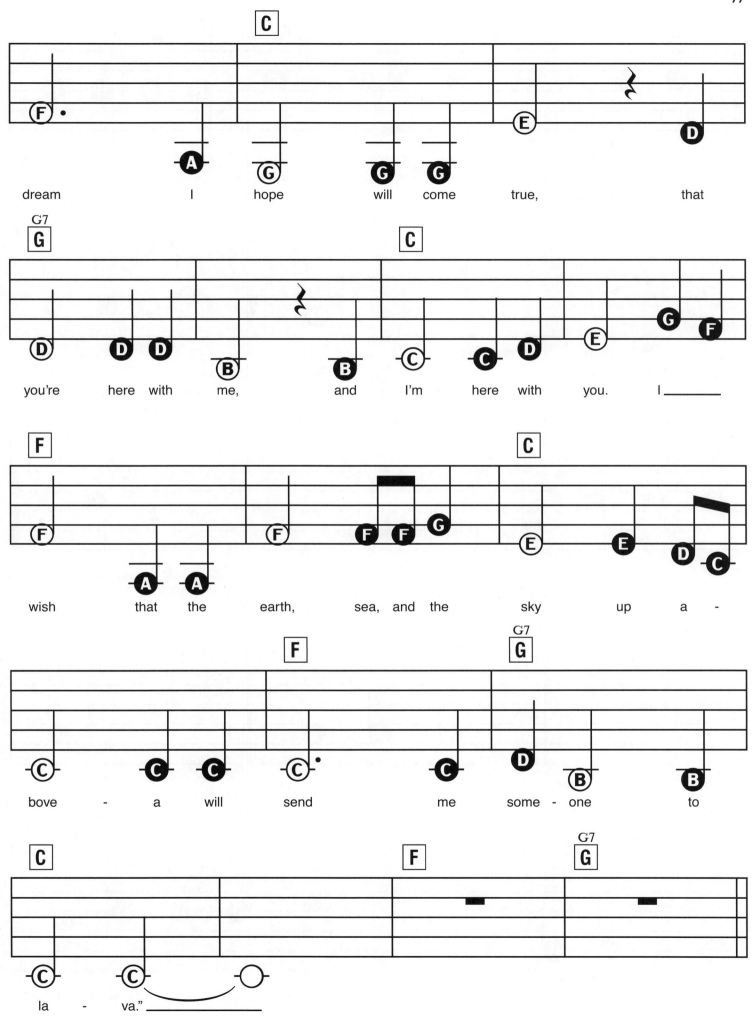

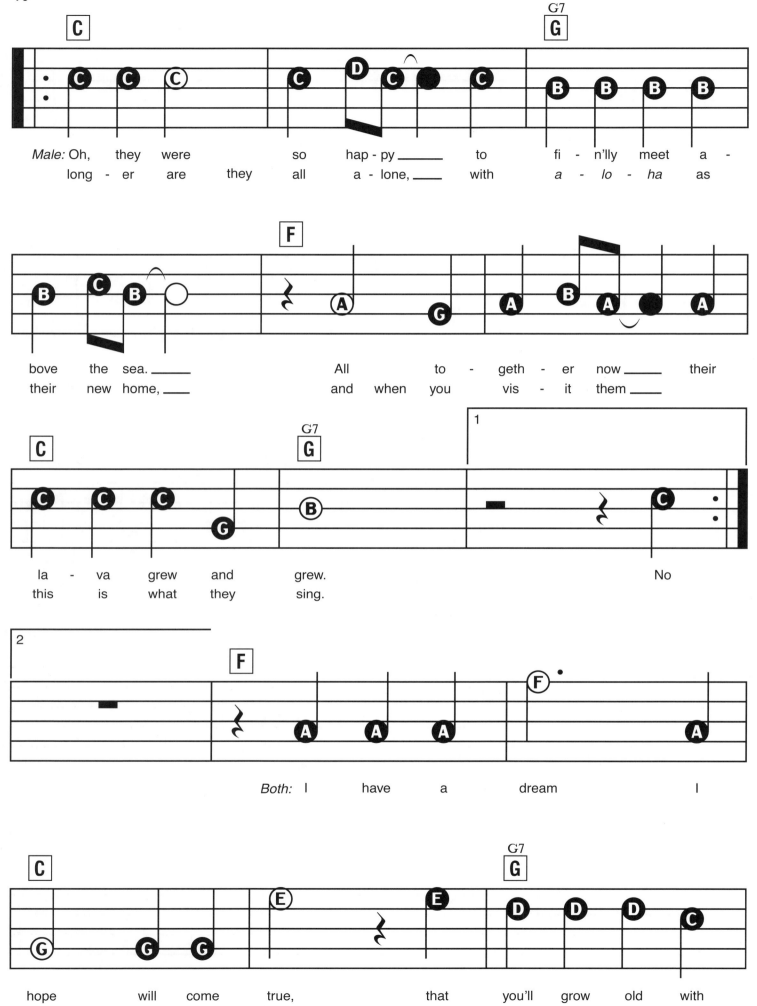

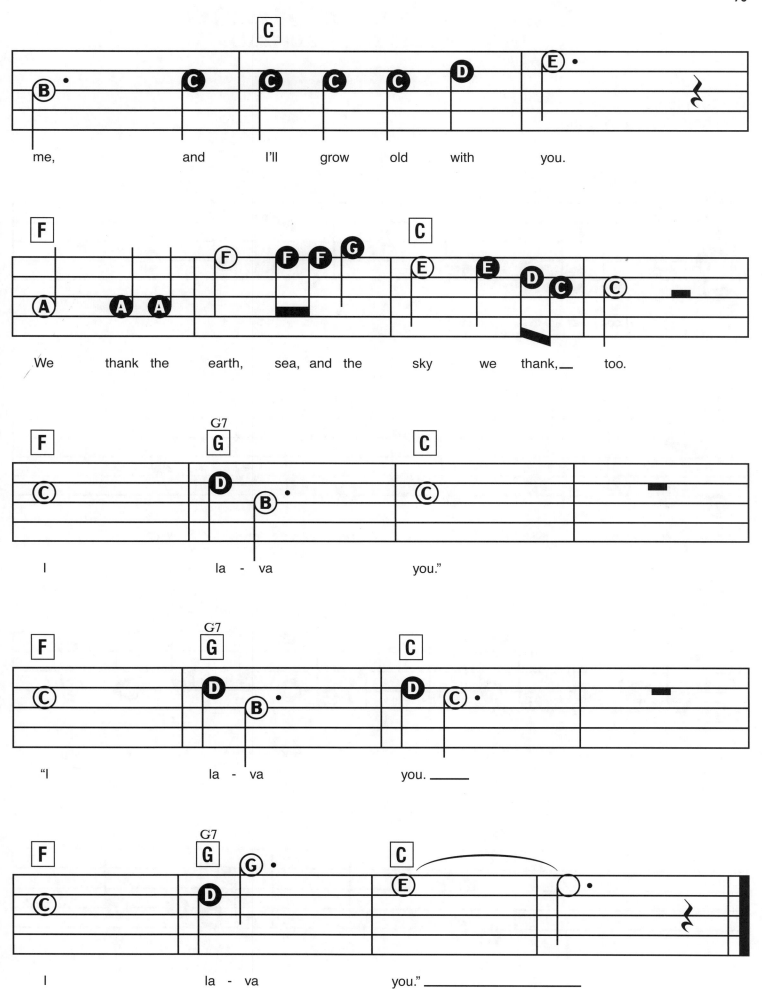

Part of Your World
from THE LITTLE MERMAID

Registration 1
Rhythm: Pops or 8-Beat

Music by Alan Menken
Lyrics by Howard Ashman

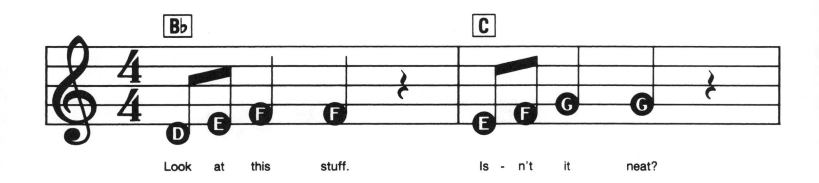

Look at this stuff. Is - n't it neat?

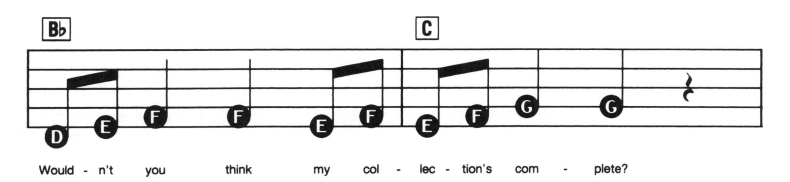

Would - n't you think my col - lec - tion's com - plete?

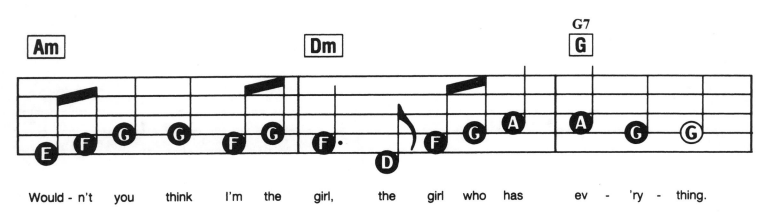

Would - n't you think I'm the girl, the girl who has ev - 'ry - thing.

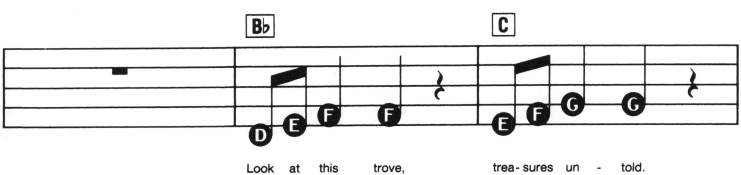

Look at this trove, trea - sures un - told.

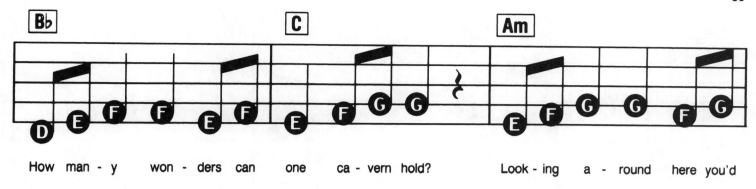

How man - y won - ders can one ca - vern hold? Look - ing a - round here you'd

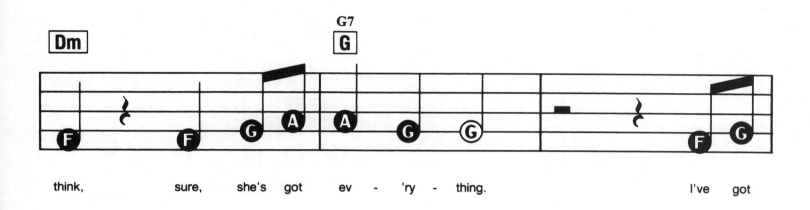

think, sure, she's got ev - 'ry - thing. I've got

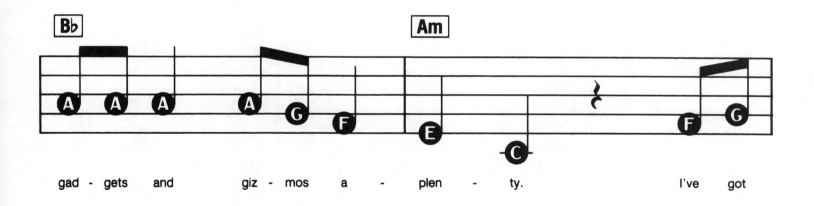

gad - gets and giz - mos a - plen - ty. I've got

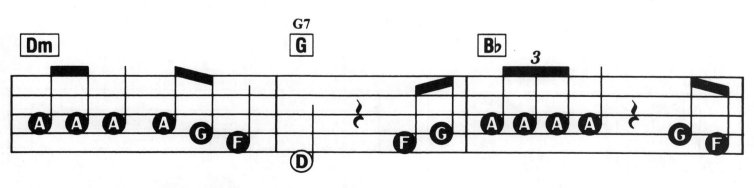

who - zits and what - zits ga - lore. You want thing - a - ma - bobs, I've got

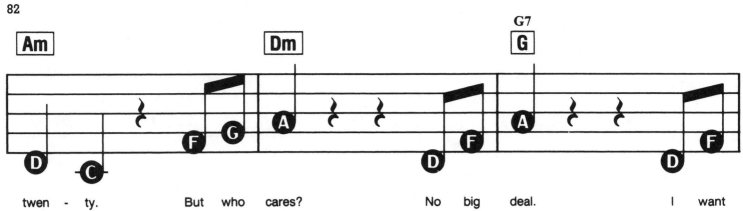

twen - ty.   But who cares?   No big deal.   I want

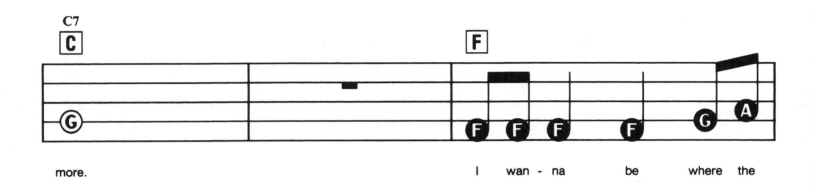

more.   I wan - na be where the

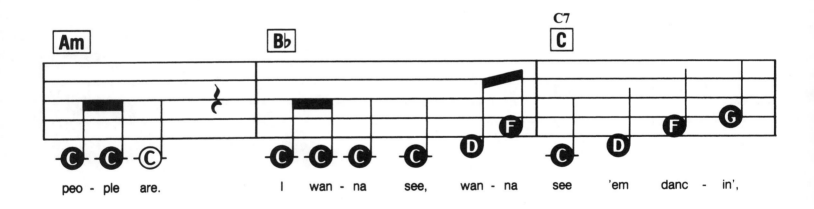

peo - ple are.   I wan - na see, wan - na see 'em danc - in',

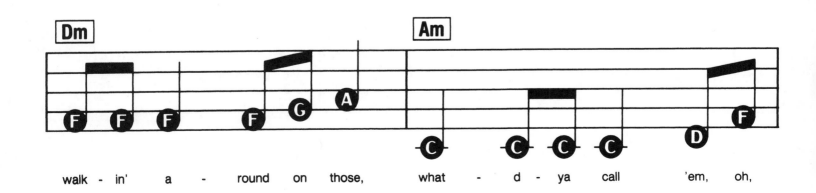

walk - in' a - round on those,   what - d - ya call 'em, oh,

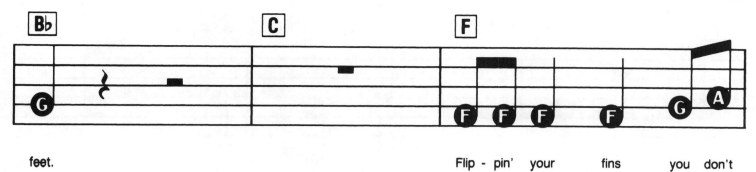

feet.　　　　　　　　　　Flip - pin' your　　fins　　you don't

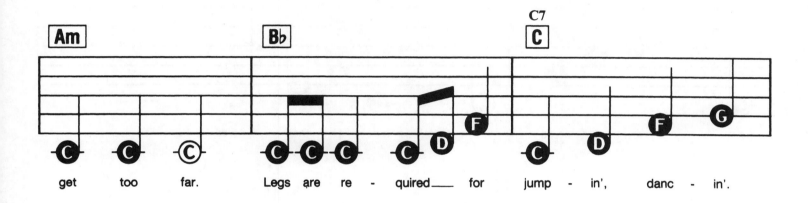

get　　too　　far.　　Legs are re - quired___ for　jump - in',　danc - in'.

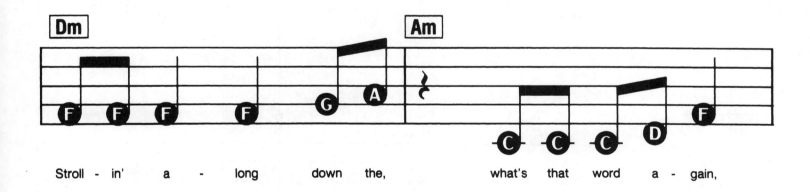

Stroll - in' a - long　down　the,　　　　what's　that　word　a - gain,

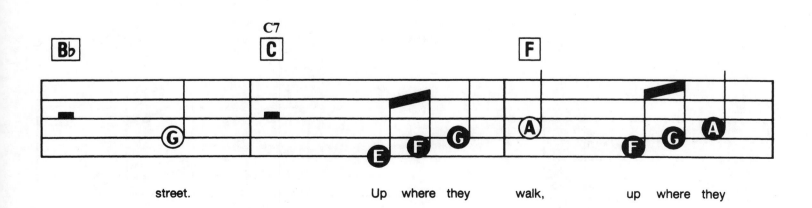

street.　　　　Up　where they　　walk,　　up　where they

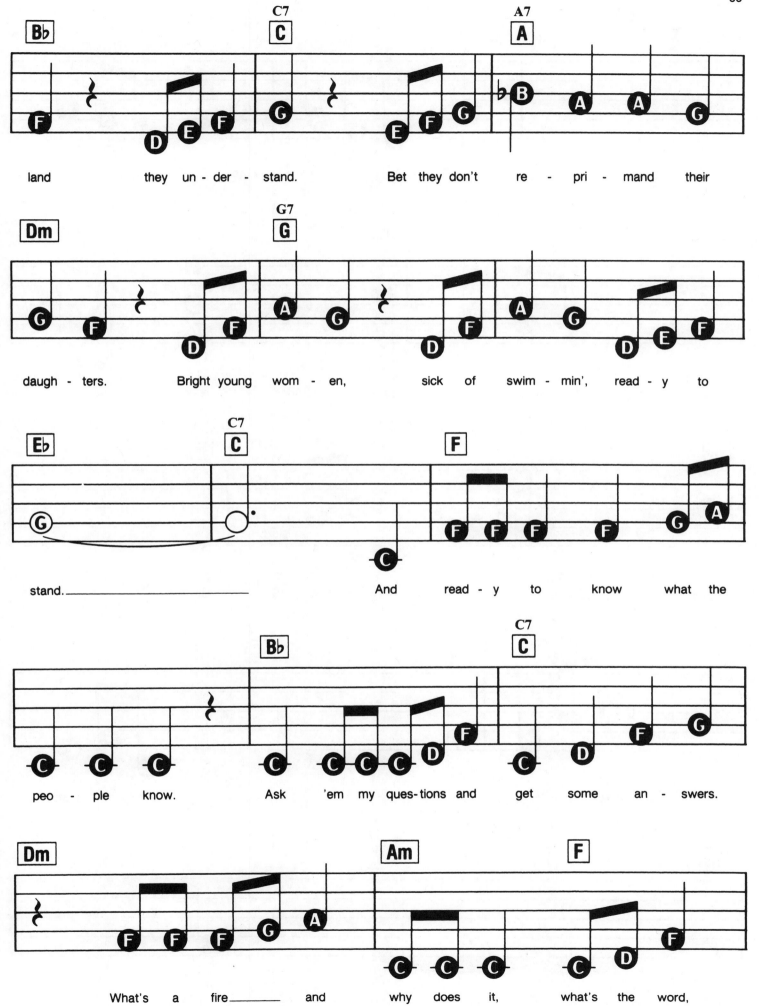

burn.   When's it my turn?   Would-n't I

love,   love to ex - plore that   shore   up a -

bove,_____   out of the sea.

Wish I could be   part of that

world._____

Reflection
from MULAN

Registration 10
Rhythm: Ballad

Music by Matthew Wilder
Lyrics by David Zippel

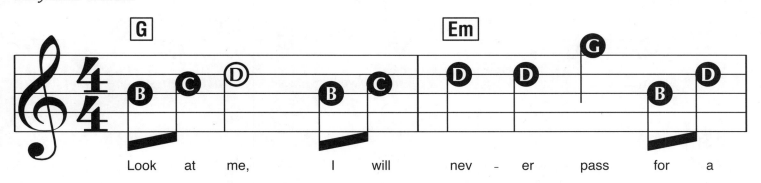

Look at me, I will nev - er pass for a

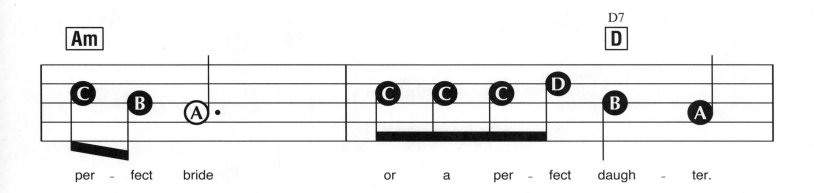

per - fect bride or a per - fect daugh - ter.

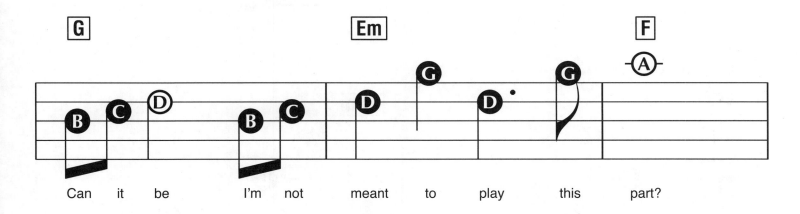

Can it be I'm not meant to play this part?

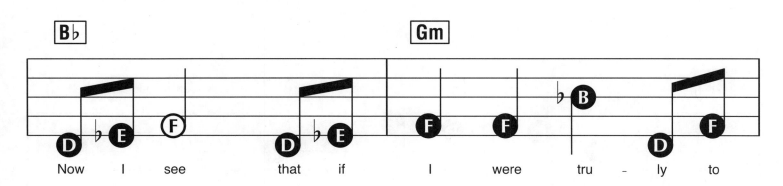

Now I see that if I were tru - ly to

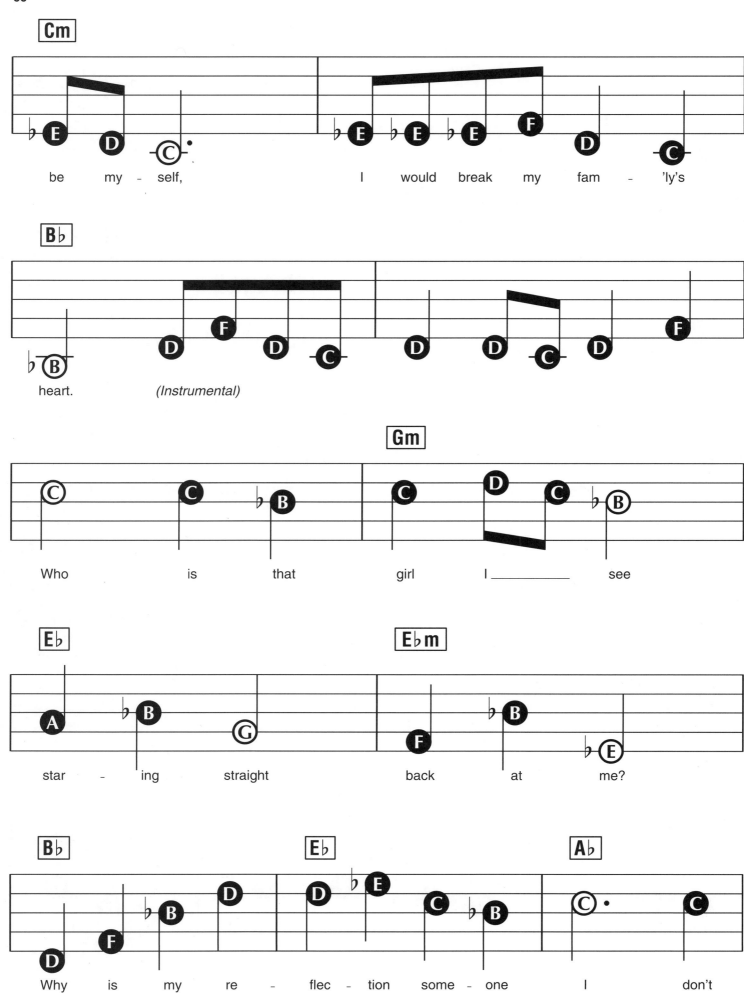

89

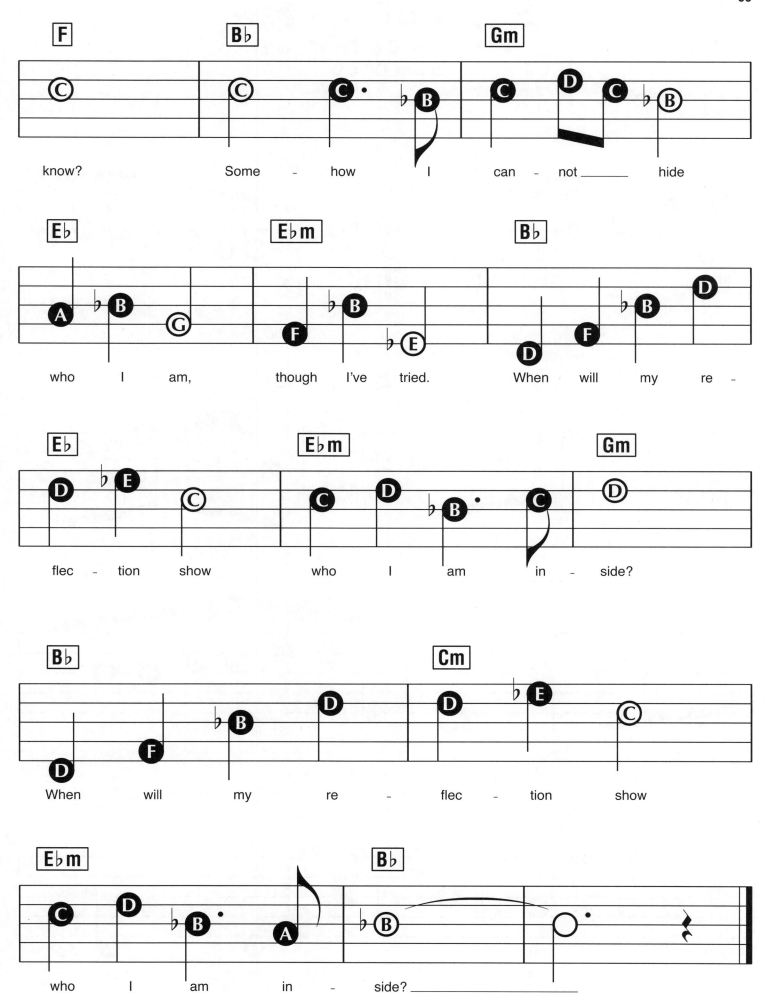

Remember Me
(Ernesto de la Cruz)
from COCO

Registration 4
Rhythm: Calypso or Pop

Music and Lyrics by Kristen Anderson-Lopez
and Robert Lopez

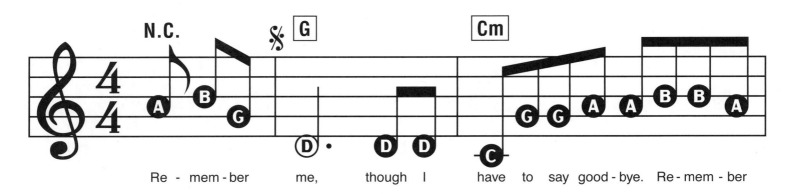

Re - mem - ber me, though I have to say good - bye. Re - mem - ber

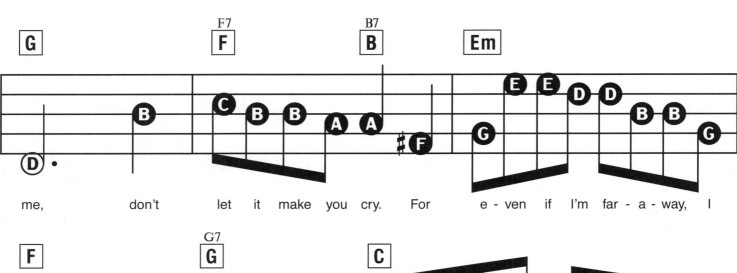

me, don't let it make you cry. For e - ven if I'm far - a - way, I

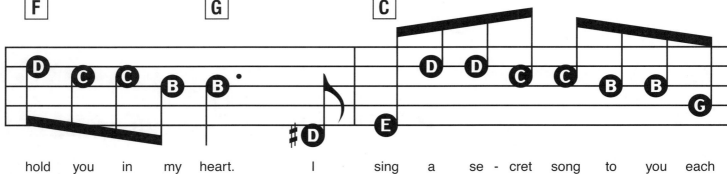

hold you in my heart. I sing a se - cret song to you each

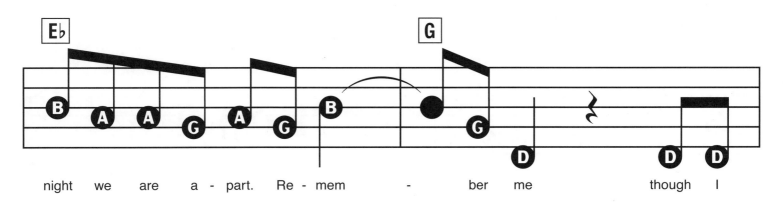

night we are a - part. Re - mem - ber me though I

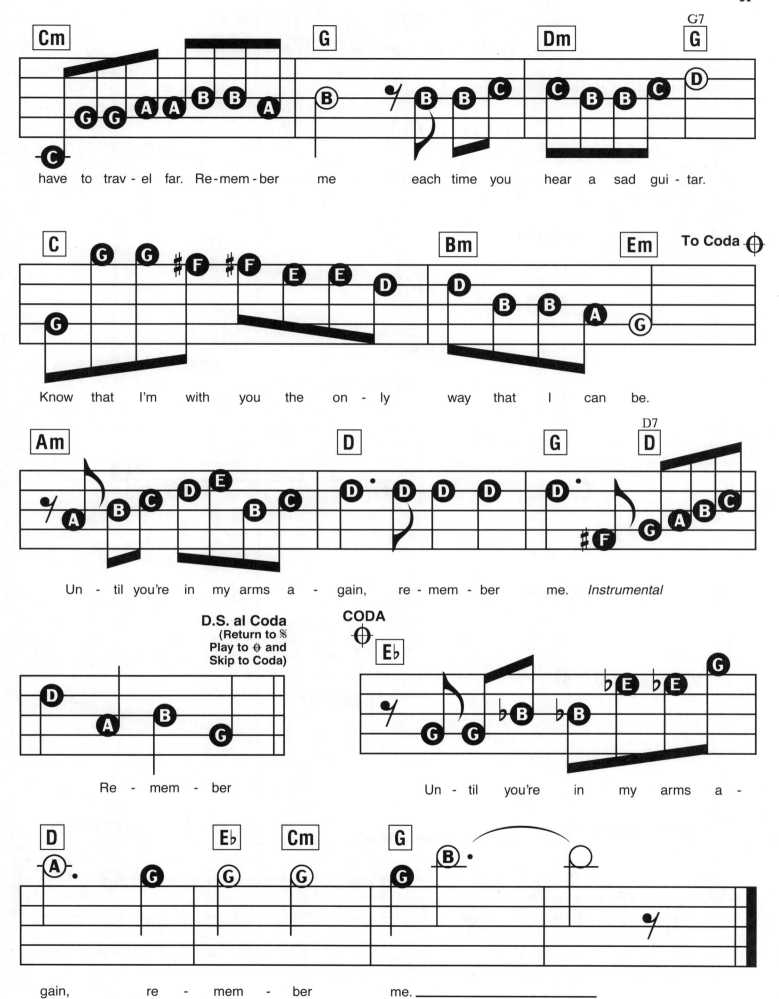

Something There
from BEAUTY AND THE BEAST

Registration 7
Rhythm: 8-Beat or Pops

Music by Alan Menken
Lyrics by Howard Ashman

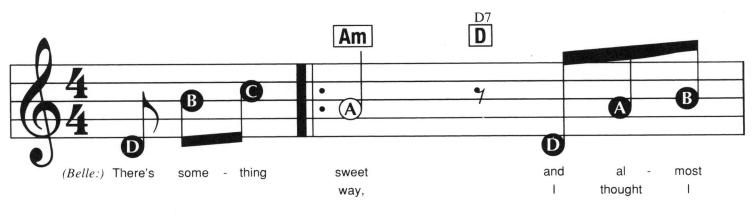

(Belle:) There's some - thing sweet
way, and al - most
I thought I

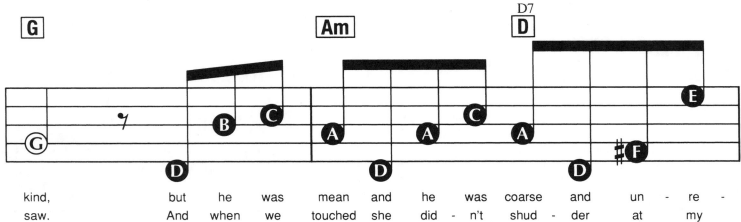

kind, but he was mean and he was coarse and un - re -
saw. And when we touched she did - n't shud - der at my

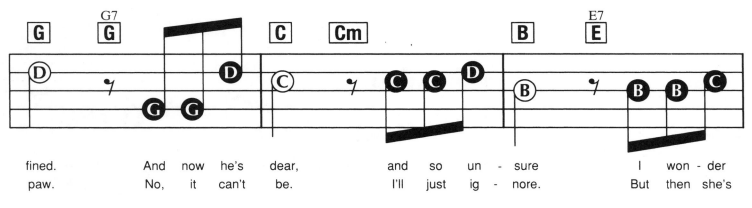

fined. And now he's dear, and so un - sure I won - der
paw. No, it can't be. I'll just ig - nore. But then she's

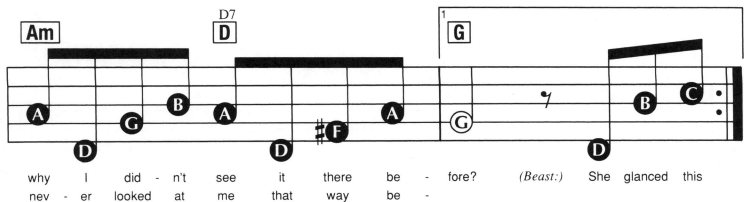

why I did - n't see it there be - fore? (Beast:) She glanced this
nev - er looked at me that way be -

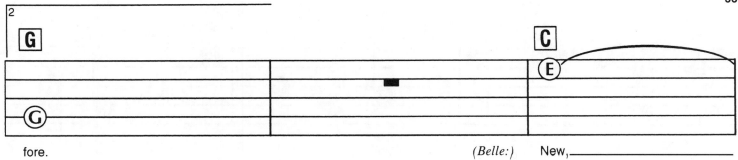

fore.   *(Belle:)*   New,_____

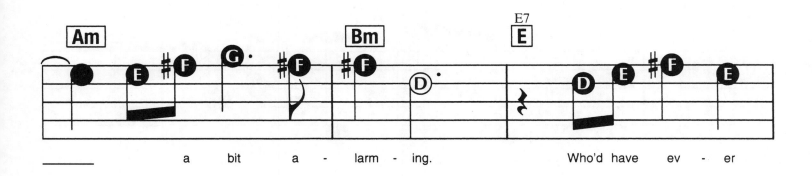

_____   a   bit   a - larm - ing.   Who'd   have   ev - er

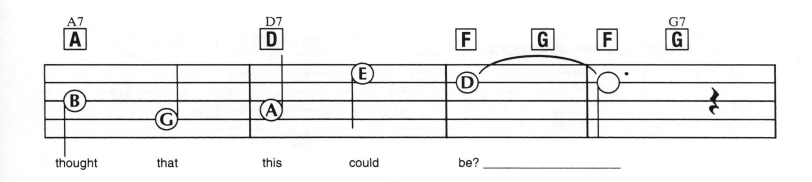

thought   that   this   could   be? _____

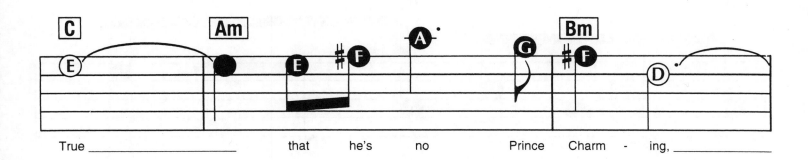

True _____   that   he's   no   Prince   Charm - ing, _____

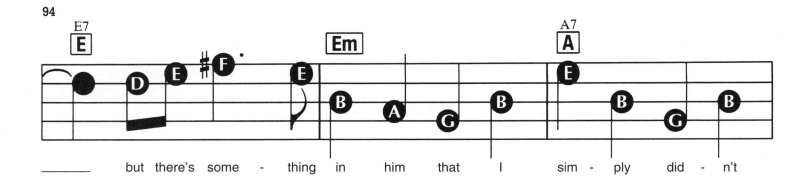

but there's some - thing in him that I sim - ply did - n't

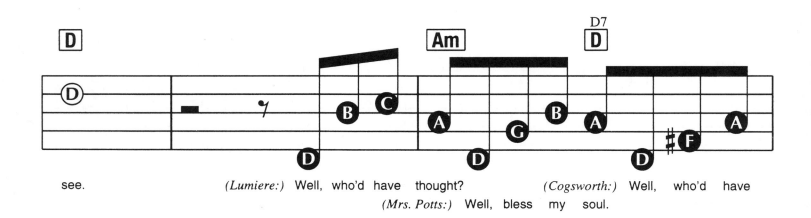

see. *(Lumiere:)* Well, who'd have thought? *(Cogsworth:)* Well, who'd have

(Mrs. Potts:) Well, bless my soul.

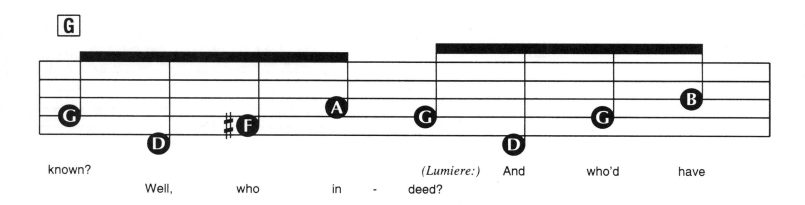

known? *(Lumiere:)* And who'd have

Well, who in - deed?

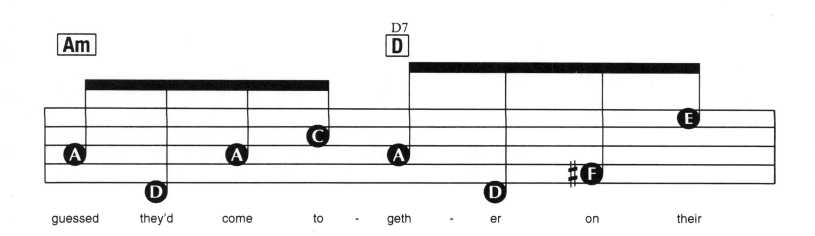

guessed they'd come to - geth - er on their

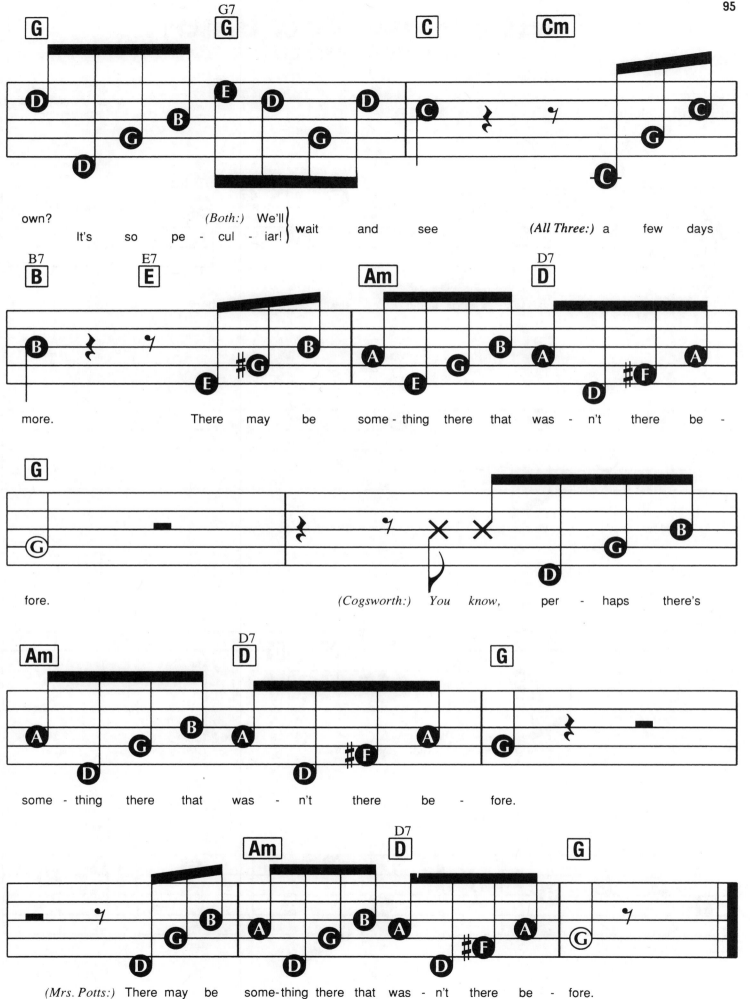

That's How You Know
from ENCHANTED

Registration 5
Rhythm: Calypso

Music by Alan Menken
Lyrics by Stephen Schwartz

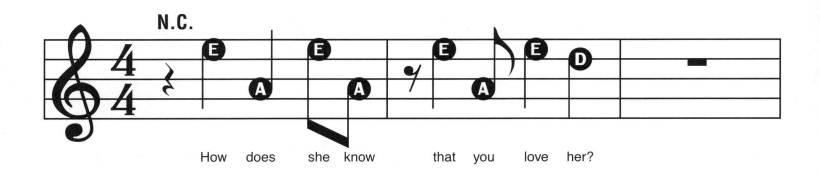

How does she know that you love her?

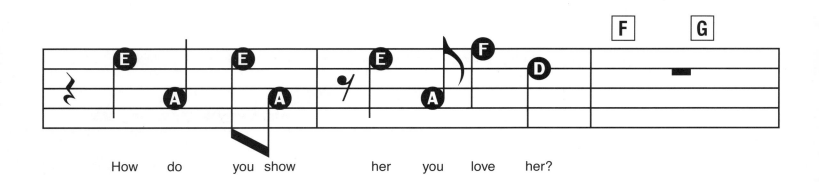

How do you show her you love her?

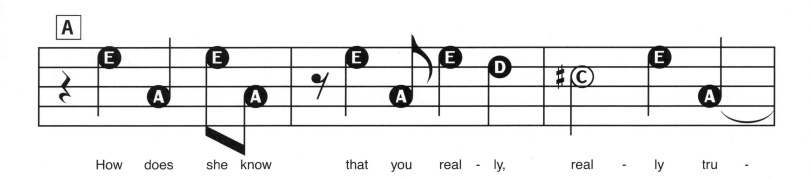

How does she know that you real - ly, real - ly tru -

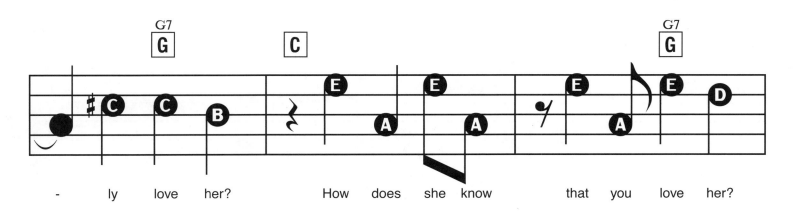

- ly love her? How does she know that you love her?

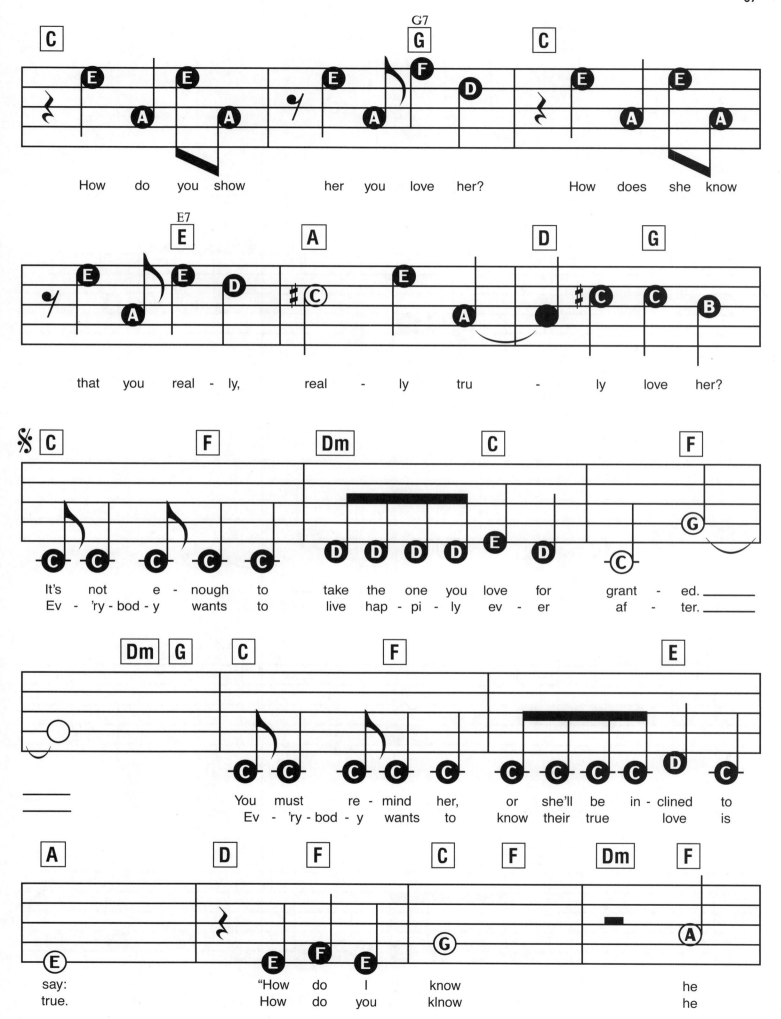

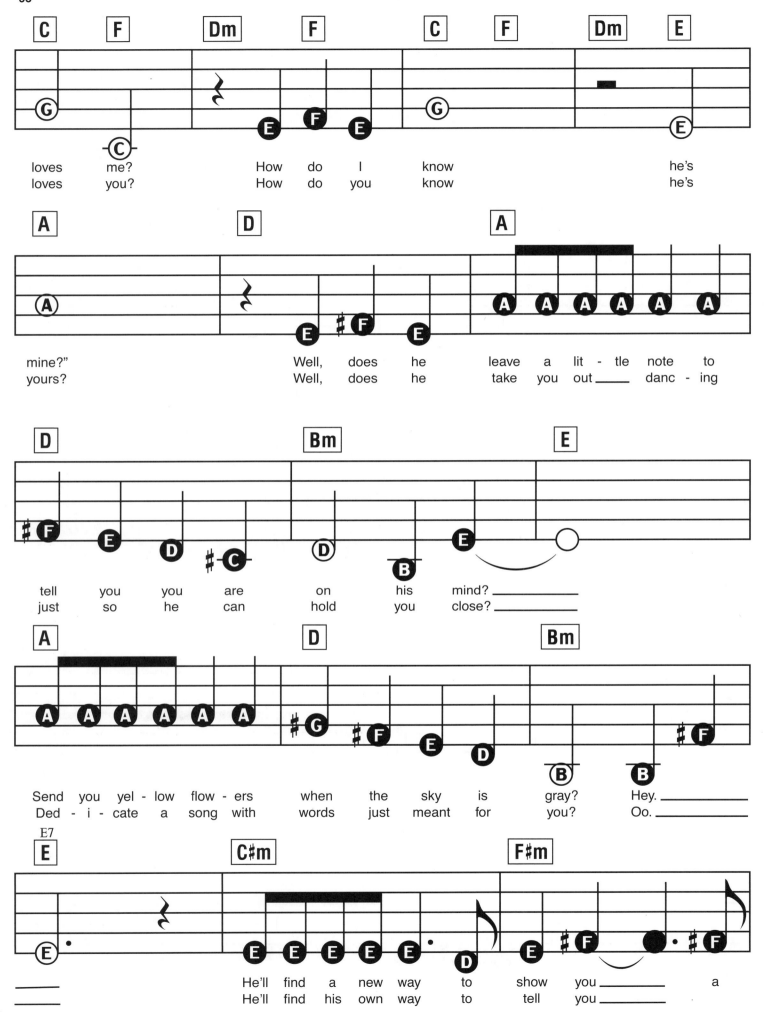

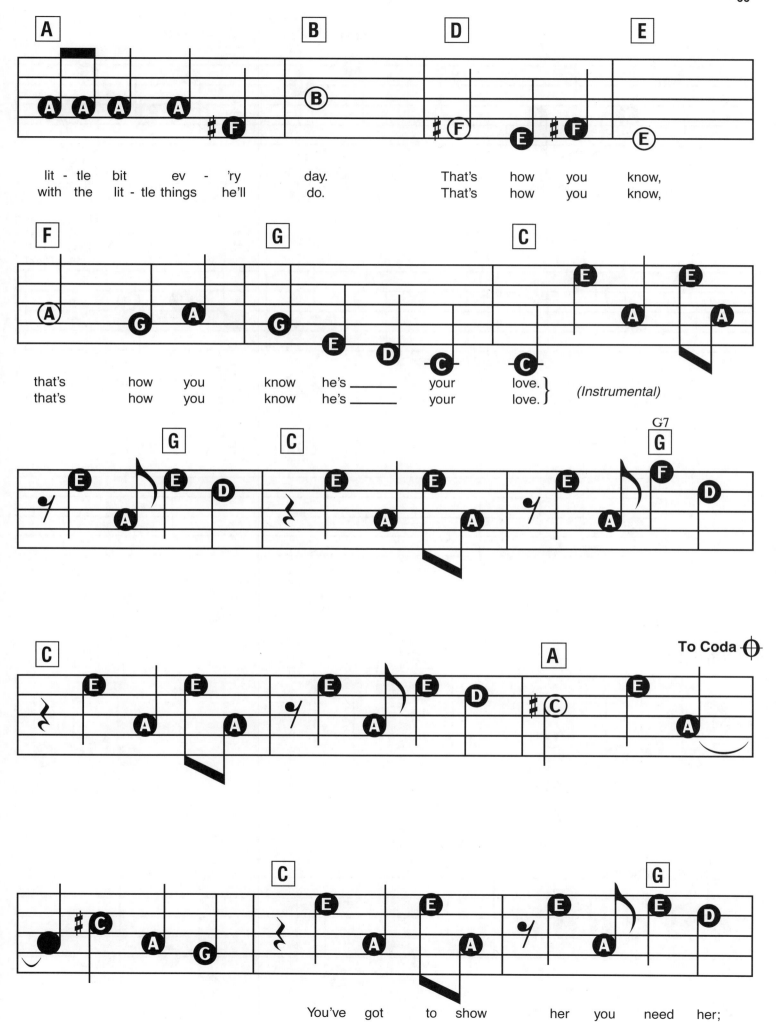

lit - tle bit ev - 'ry day. That's how you know,
with the lit - tle things he'll do. That's how you know,

that's how you know he's _____ your love. }
that's how you know he's _____ your love. } (Instrumental)

To Coda

You've got to show her you need her;

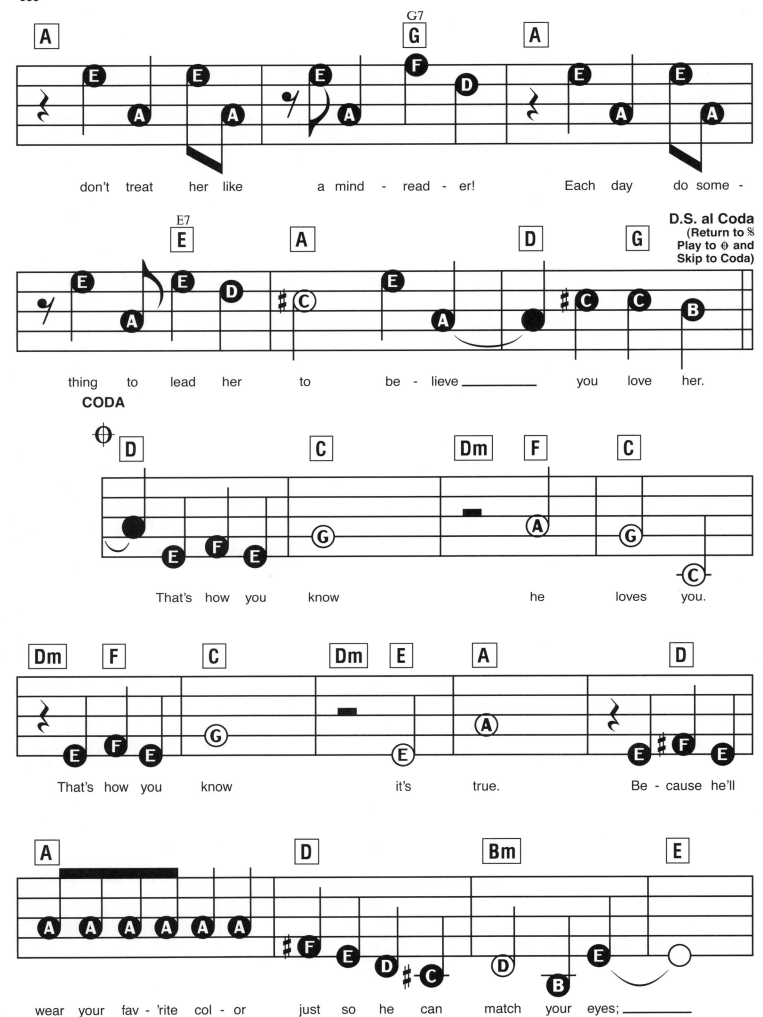

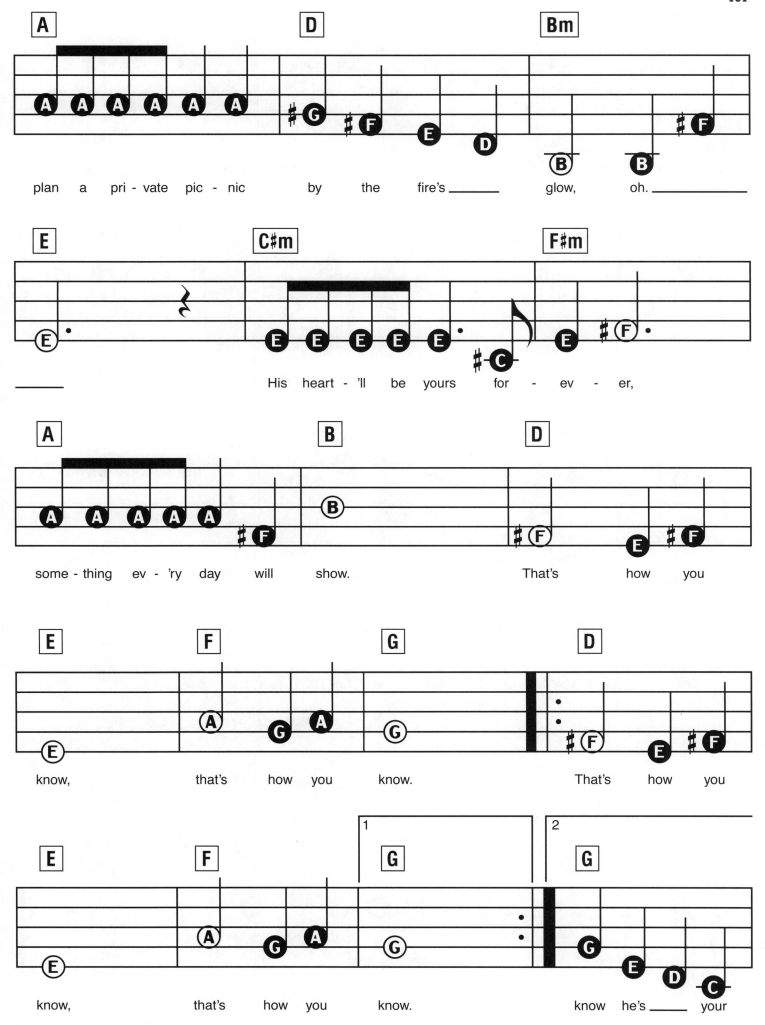

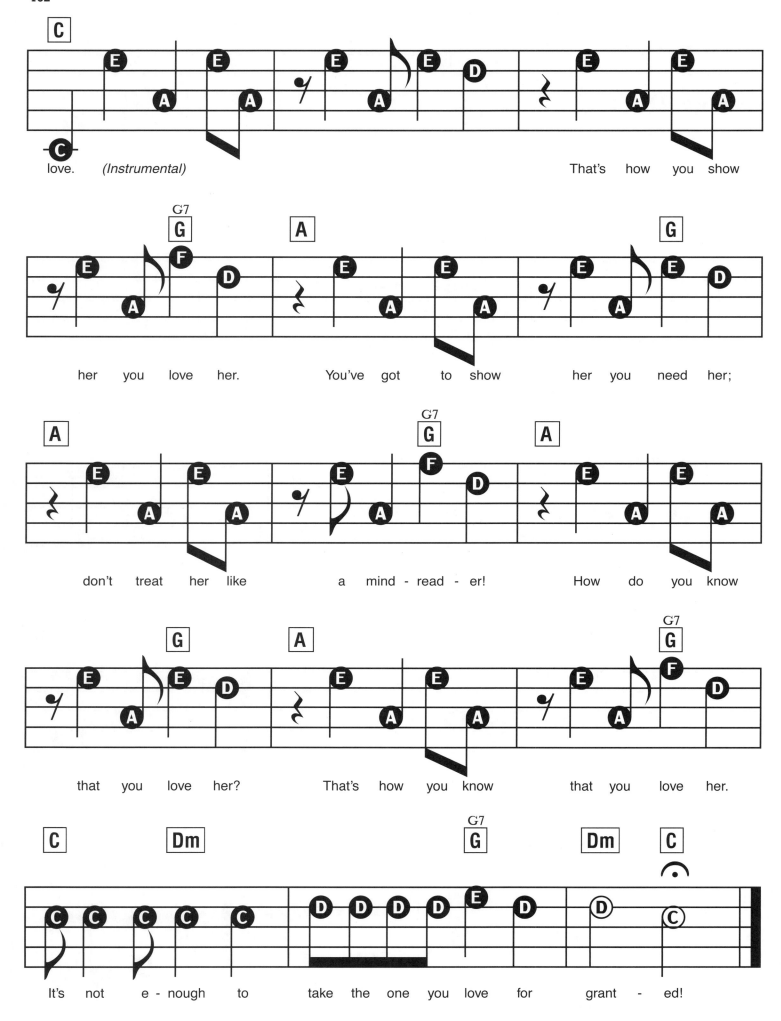

Where You Are
from MOANA

Registration 5
Rhythm: Calypso or Pop

Music by Lin-Manuel Miranda,
Opetaia Foa'i and Mark Mancina
Lyrics by Lin-Manuel Miranda

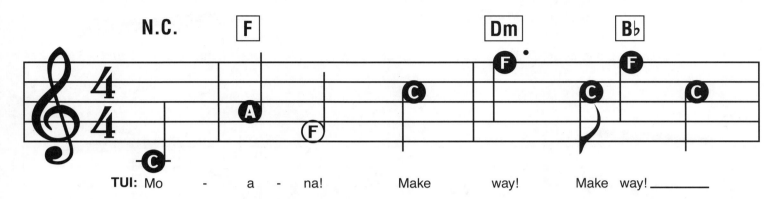

TUI: Mo - a - na! Make way! Make way! _____

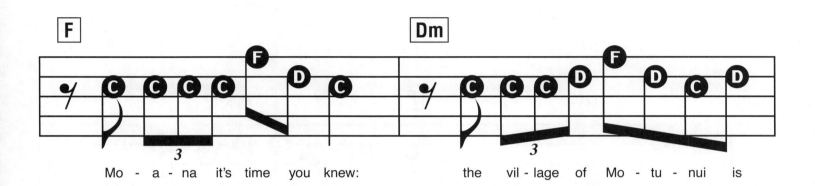

Mo - a - na it's time you knew: the vil - lage of Mo - tu - nui is

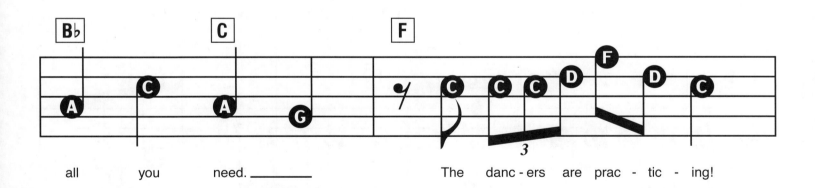

all you need. _____ The danc - ers are prac - tic - ing!

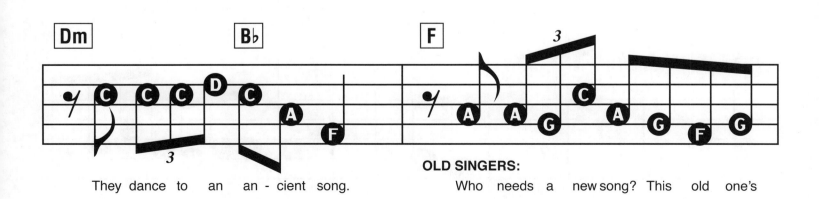

They dance to an an - cient song. OLD SINGERS: Who needs a new song? This old one's

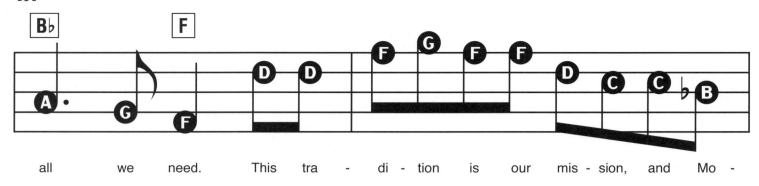

all   we   need.   This   tra - di - tion   is   our   mis - sion,   and   Mo -

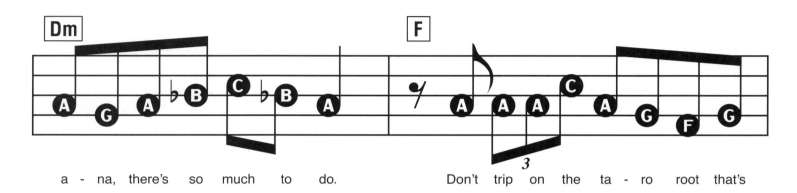

a - na,   there's   so   much   to   do.   Don't   trip   on   the   ta - ro   root   that's

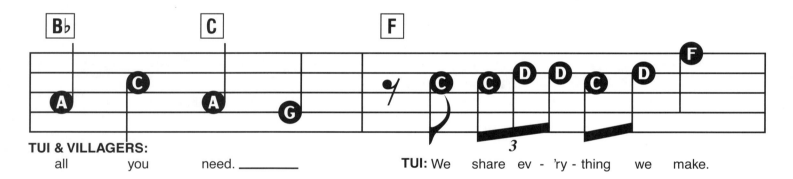

TUI & VILLAGERS:
all   you   need. _____   **TUI:** We   share   ev - 'ry - thing   we   make.

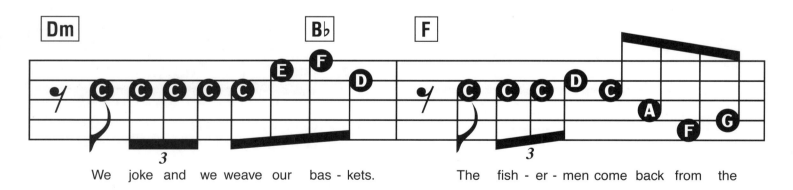

We   joke   and   we   weave   our   bas - kets.   The   fish - er - men   come   back   from   the

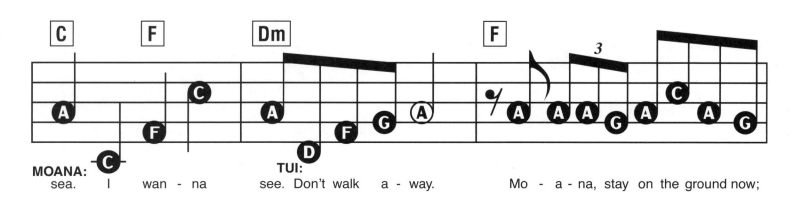

MOANA:
sea.   I   wan - na   see. Don't   walk   a - way.   Mo - a - na, stay   on   the   ground   now;
TUI:

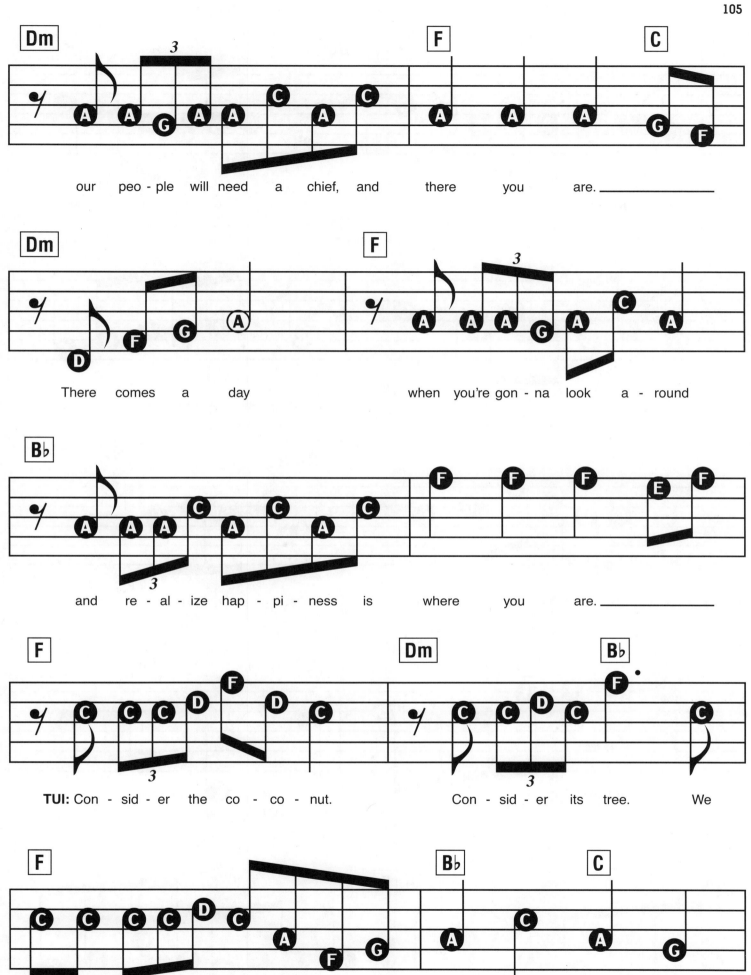

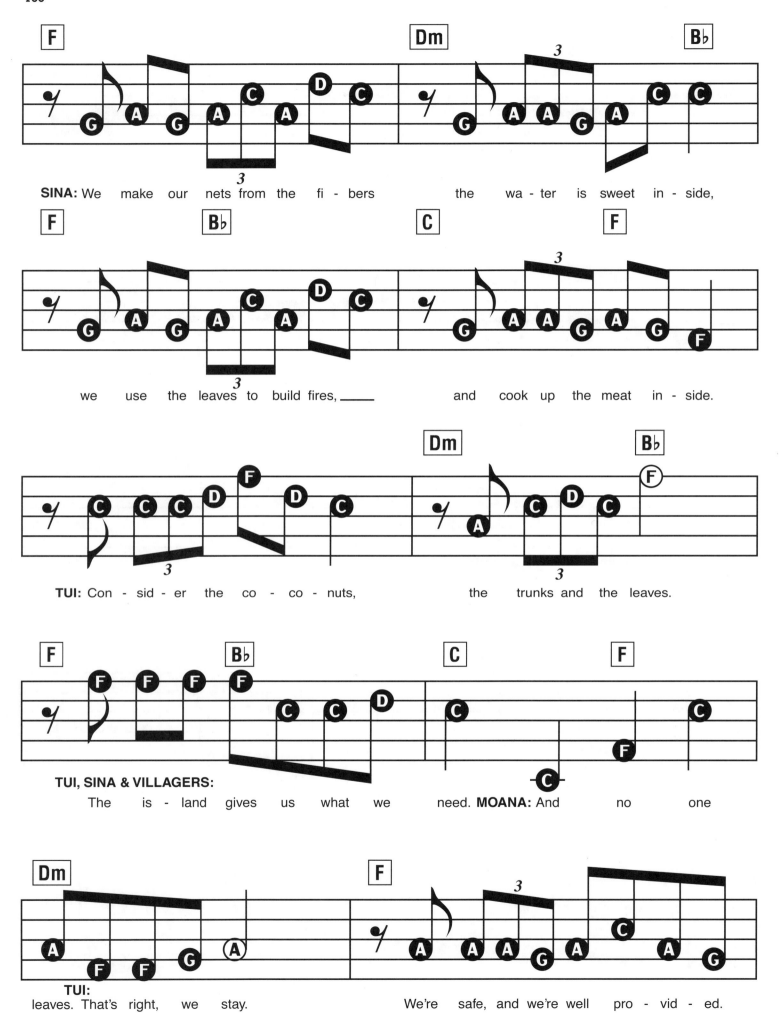

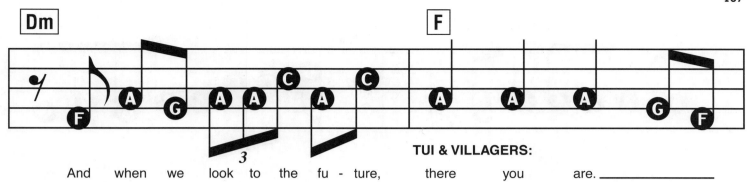

TUI & VILLAGERS:
And when we look to the fu - ture, there you are. _____

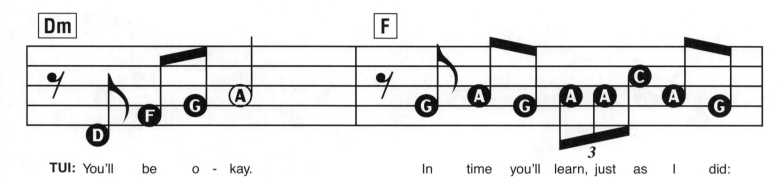

TUI: You'll be o - kay. In time you'll learn, just as I did:

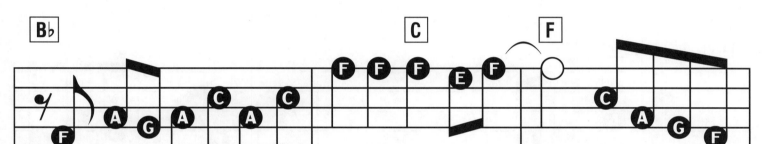

you must find hap - pi - ness right where you are. _____ *(Instrumental)*

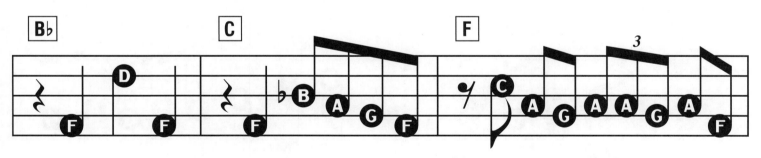

TALA: I like to dance with the wa - ter,

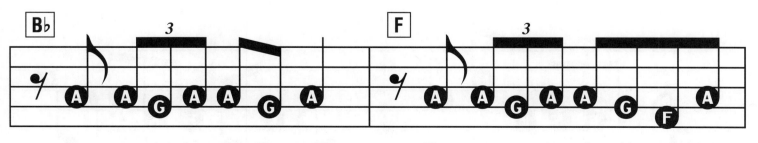

the un - der - tow and the waves. The wa - ter is mis - chie - vous, ha!

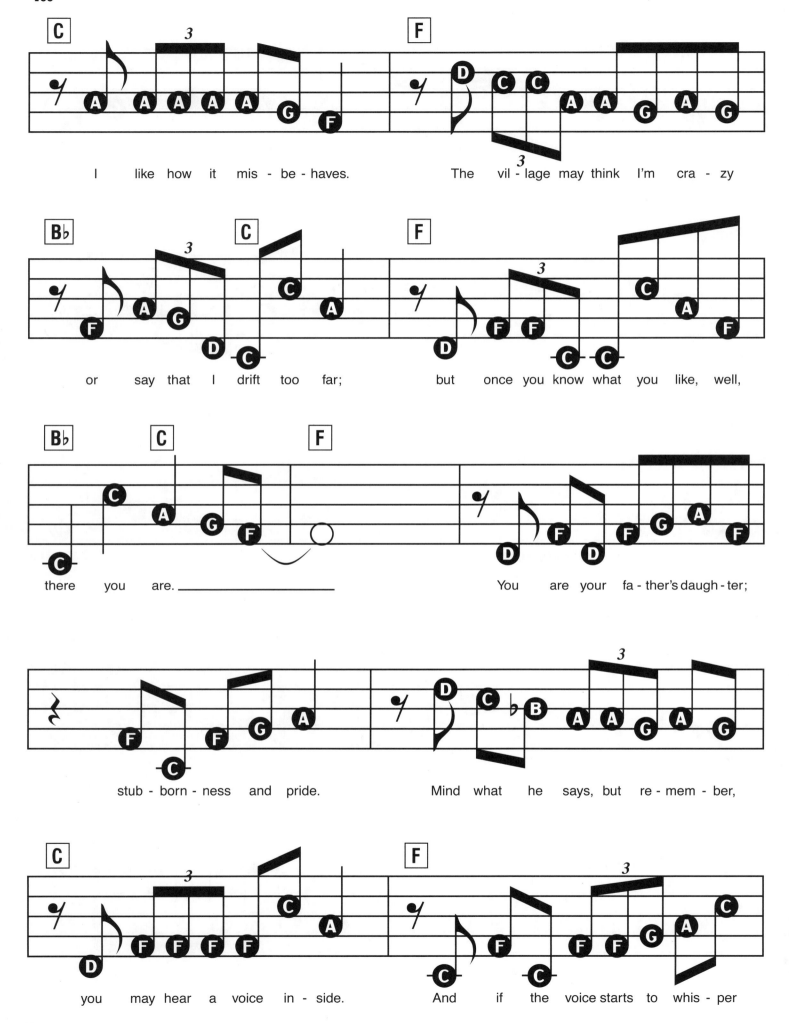

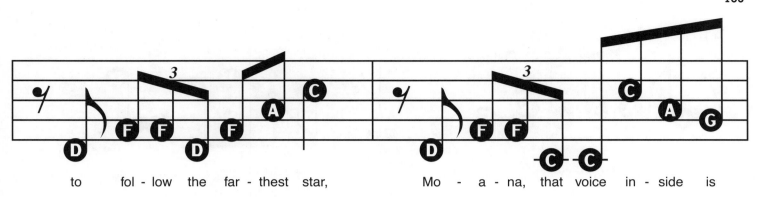

to fol - low the far - thest star,   Mo - a - na, that voice in - side is

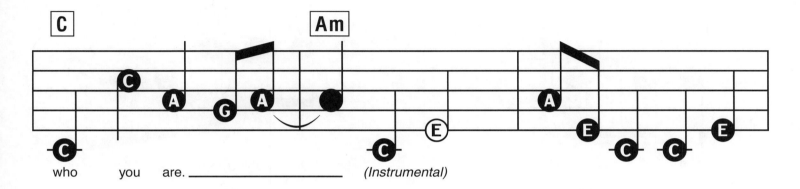

who   you   are. _____ *(Instrumental)*

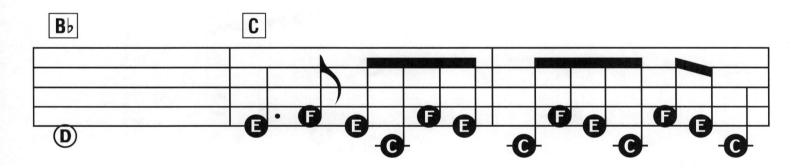

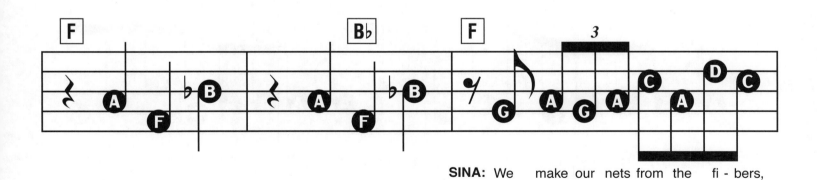

SINA: We   make our nets from the   fi - bers,

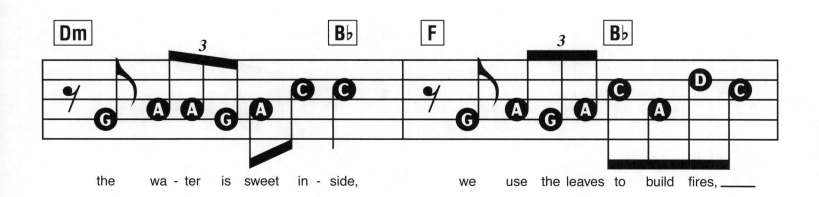

the   wa - ter   is sweet in - side,   we   use the leaves to   build fires, ____

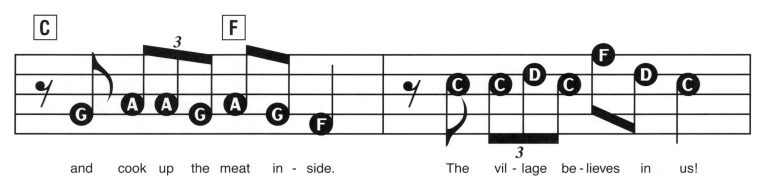

and cook up the meat in - side. The vil - lage be - lieves in us!

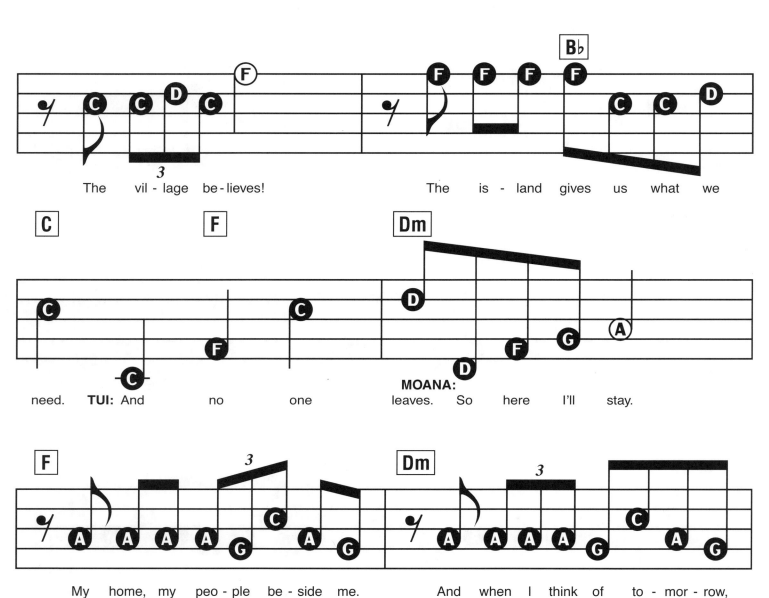

The vil - lage be - lieves! The is - land gives us what we

need. **TUI:** And no one leaves. So here I'll stay.

My home, my peo - ple be - side me. And when I think of to - mor - row,

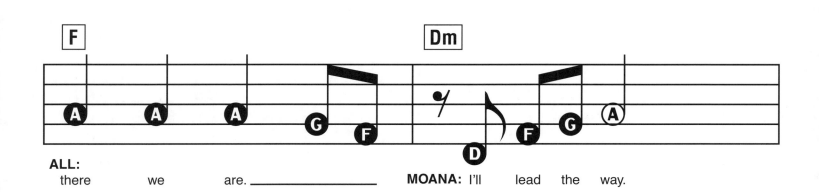

ALL:
there we are. _____ **MOANA:** I'll lead the way.

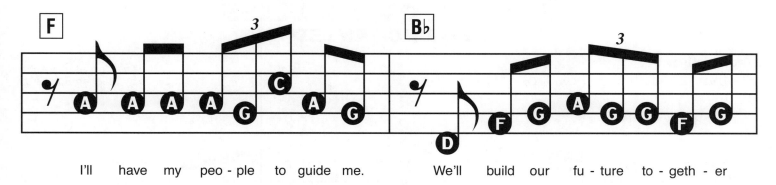

I'll have my peo - ple to guide me.
We'll build our fu - ture to - geth - er

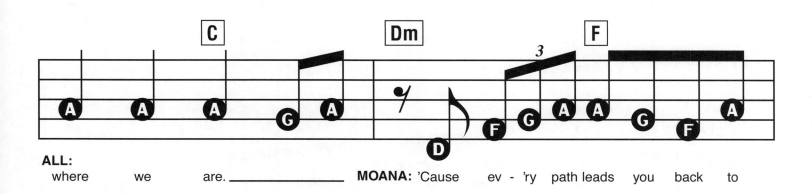

ALL:
where we are. _____
MOANA: 'Cause ev - 'ry path leads you back to

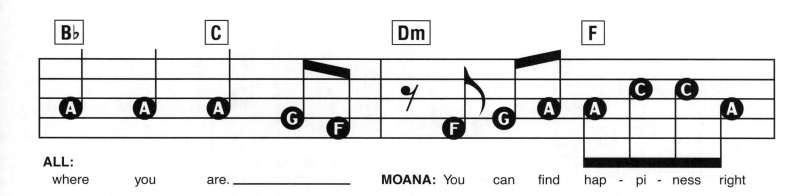

ALL:
where you are. _____
MOANA: You can find hap - pi - ness right

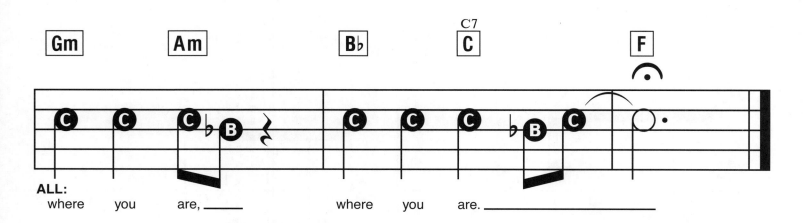

ALL:
where you are, _____
where you are. _____

True Love's Kiss
from ENCHANTED

Registration 1
Rhythm: Broadway or Fox Trot

Music by Alan Menken
Lyrics by Stephen Schwartz

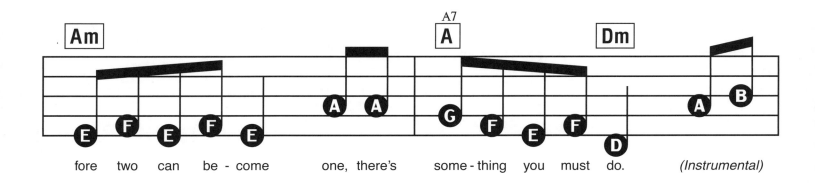

When you meet the some - one who was meant for you, be -

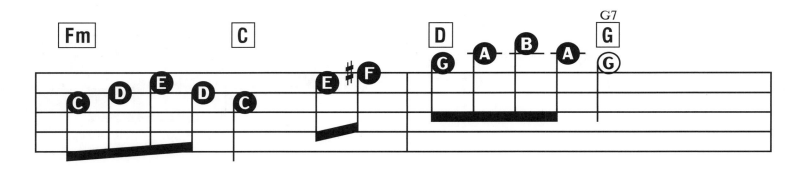

fore two can be - come one, there's some - thing you must do. *(Instrumental)*

There is some - thing sweet - er ev - 'ry - bod - y needs.

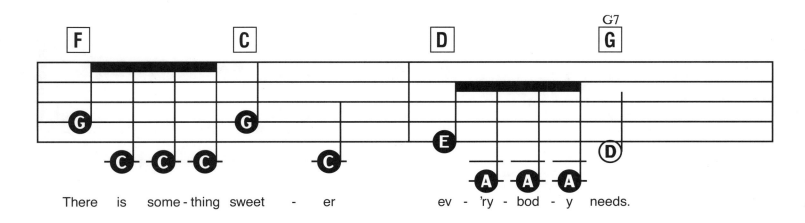

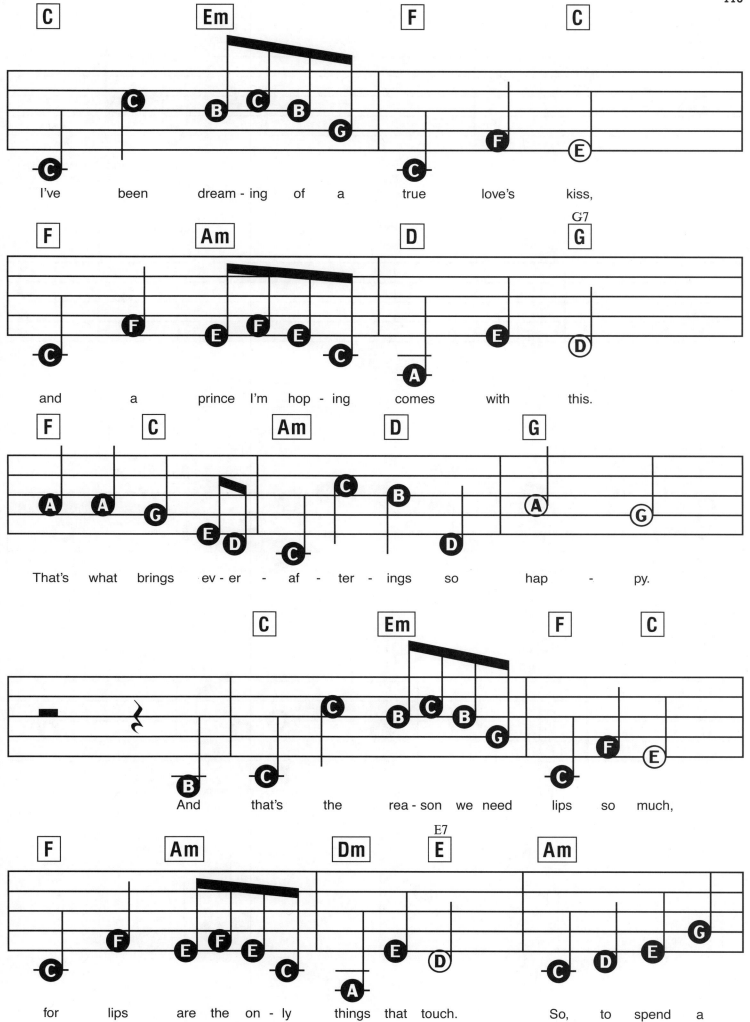

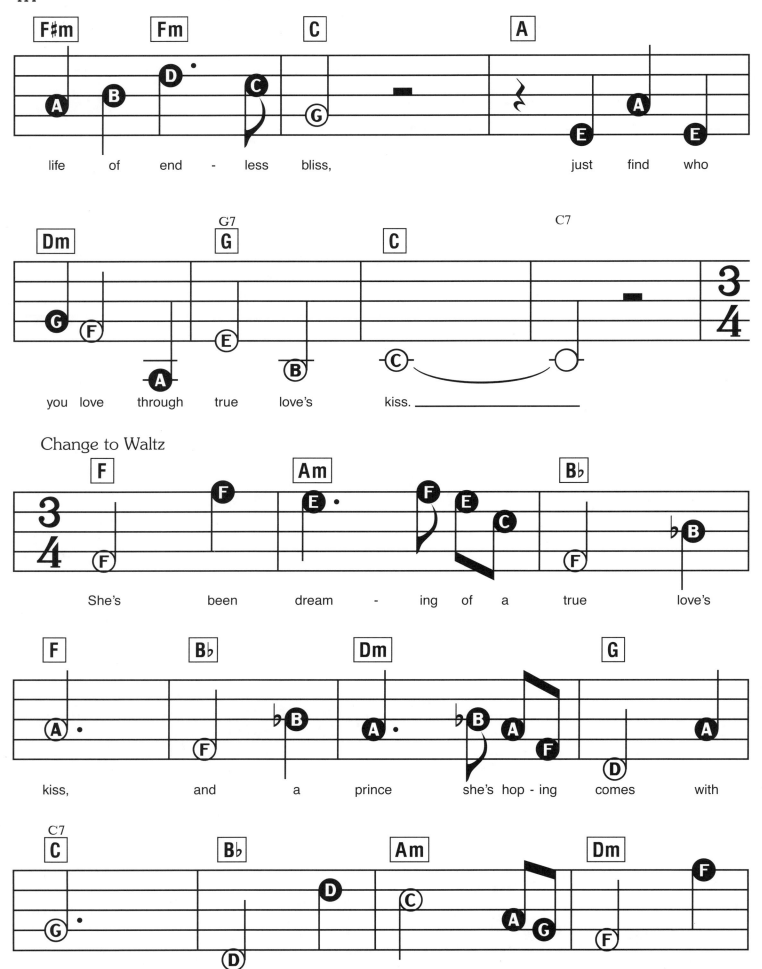

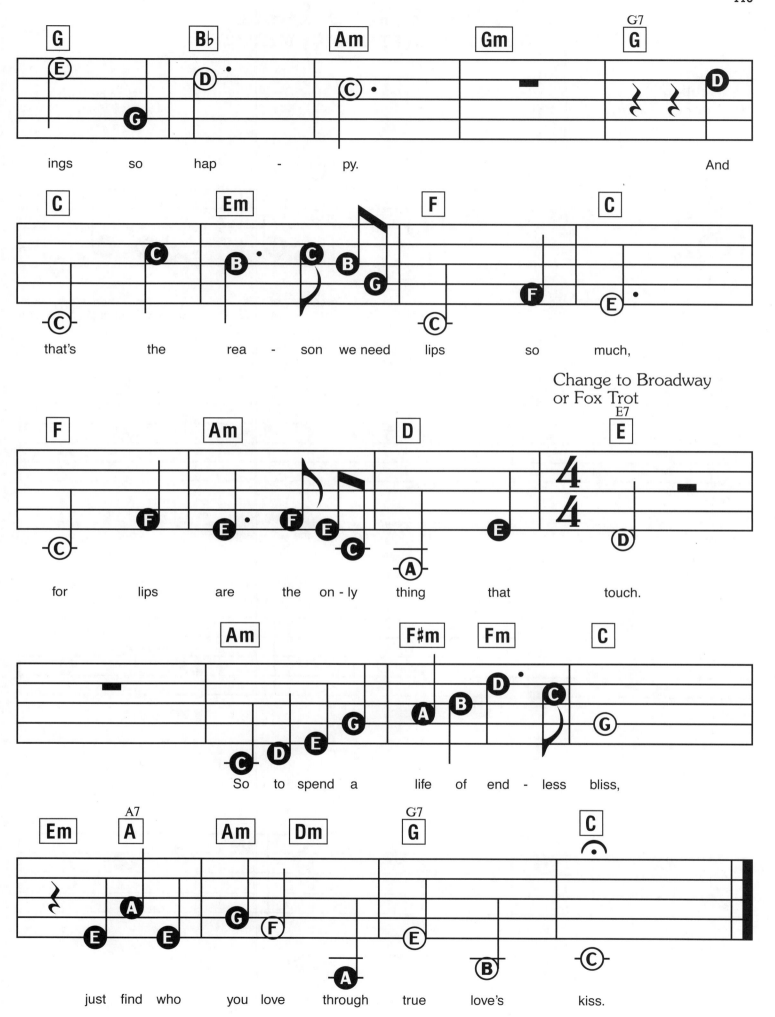

Under the Sea
from THE LITTLE MERMAID

Registration 7
Rhythm: Bossa Nova or Latin

Music by Alan Menken
Lyrics by Howard Ashman

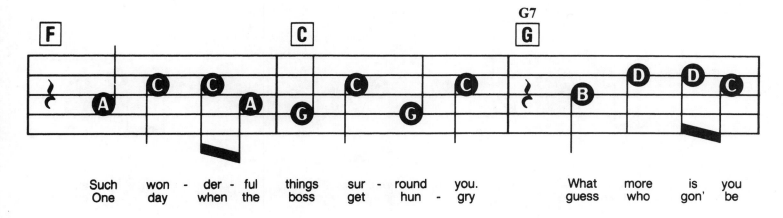

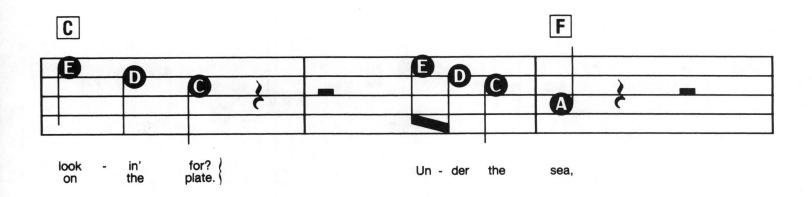

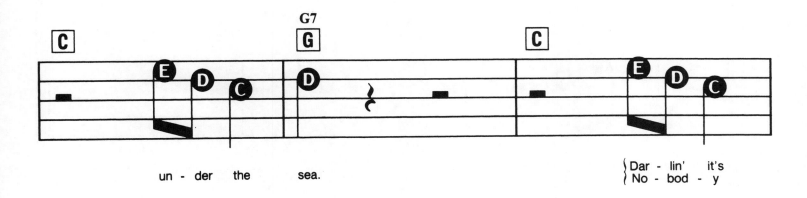

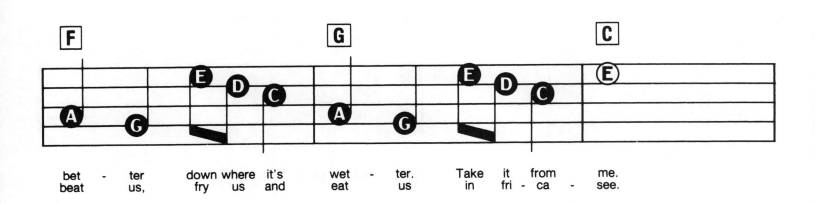

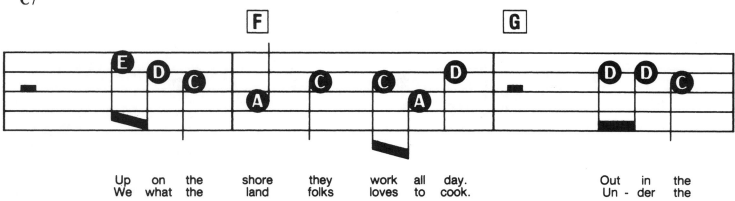

Up on the shore they work all day.
We what the land folks loves to cook.
Out in the
Un - der the

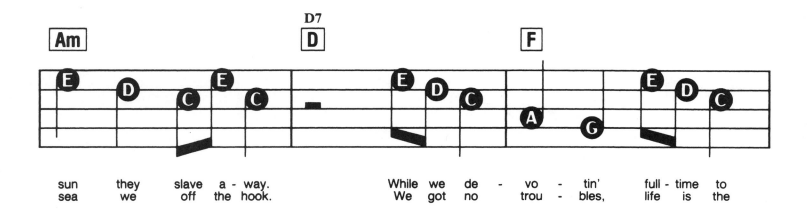

sun they slave a - way.
sea we off the hook.
While we de - vo - tin' full - time to
We got no trou - bles, life is the

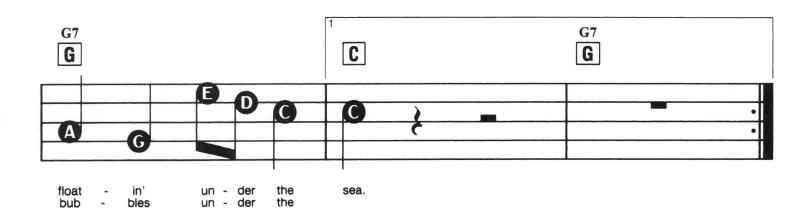

float - in' un - der the sea.
bub - bles un - der the sea.

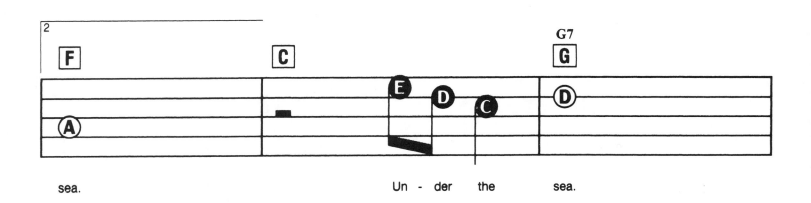

sea.
Un - der the sea.

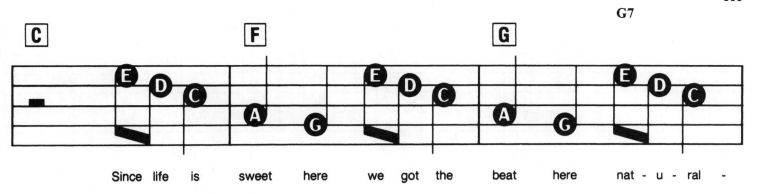

Since life is sweet here we got the beat here nat - u - ral -

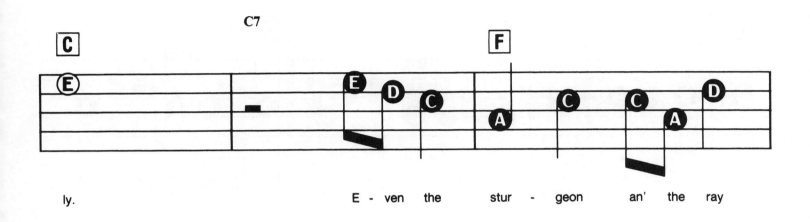

ly. E - ven the stur - geon an' the ray

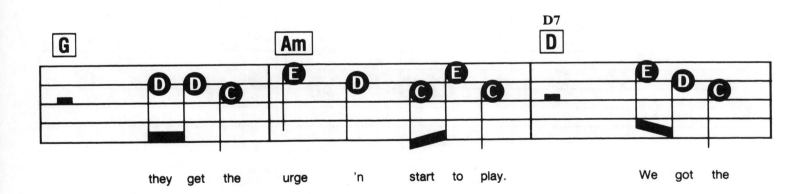

they get the urge 'n start to play. We got the

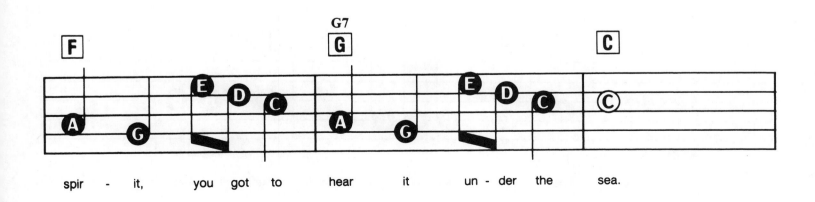

spir - it, you got to hear it un - der the sea.

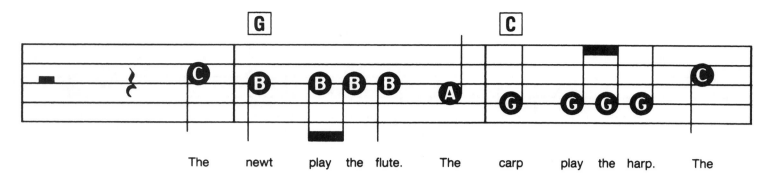

The newt play the flute. The carp play the harp. The

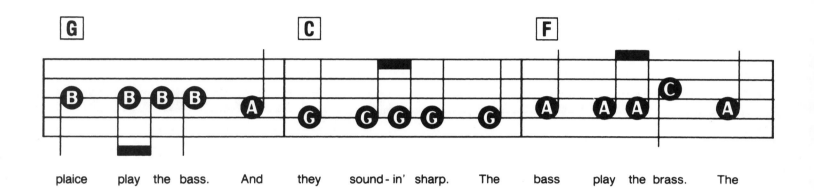

plaice play the bass. And they sound - in' sharp. The bass play the brass. The

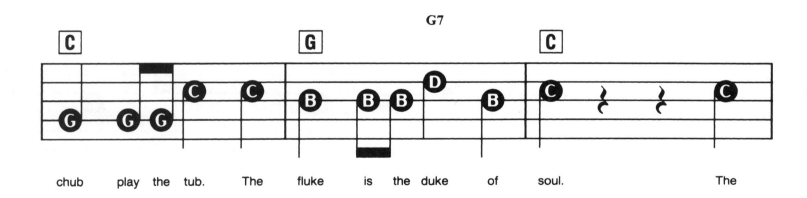

chub play the tub. The fluke is the duke of soul. The

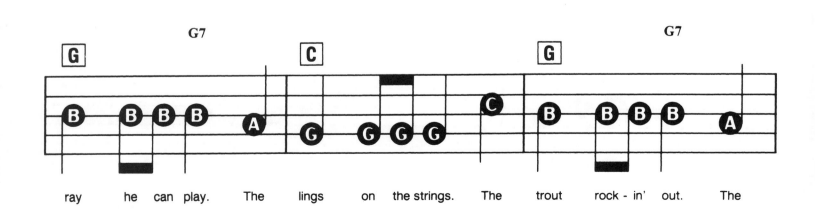

ray he can play. The lings on the strings. The trout rock - in' out. The

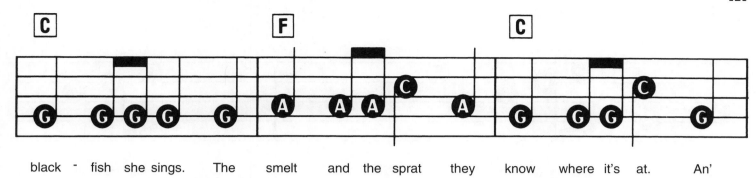

black - fish she sings. The smelt and the sprat they know where it's at. An'

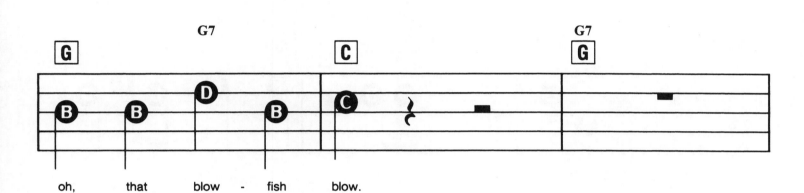

oh, that blow - fish blow.

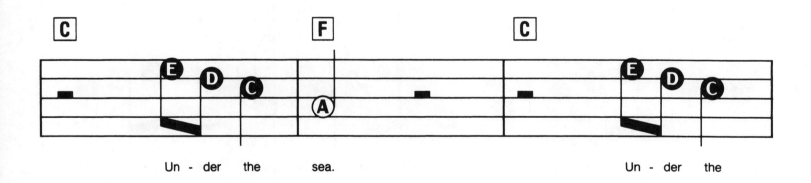

Un - der the sea. Un - der the

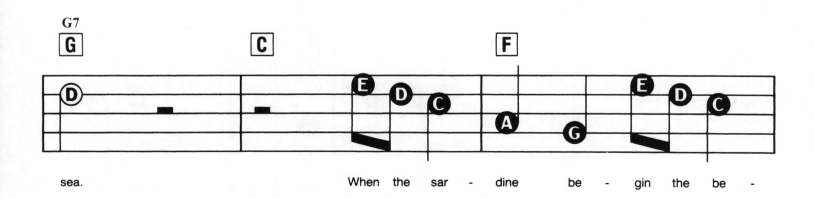

sea. When the sar - dine be - gin the be -

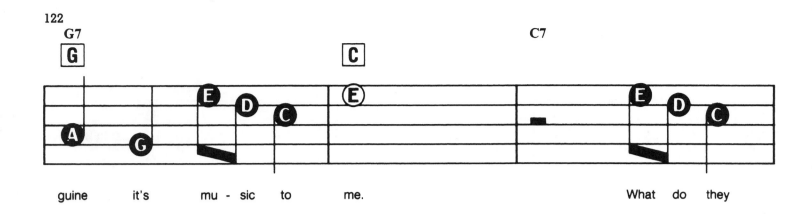

guine it's mu - sic to me. What do they

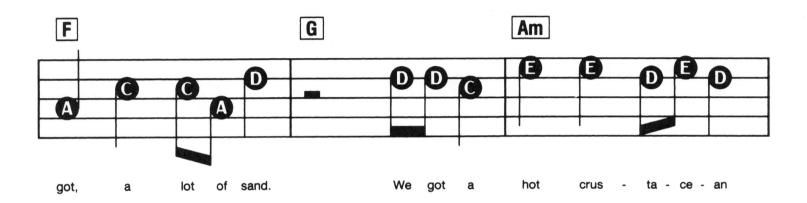

got, a lot of sand. We got a hot crus - ta - ce - an

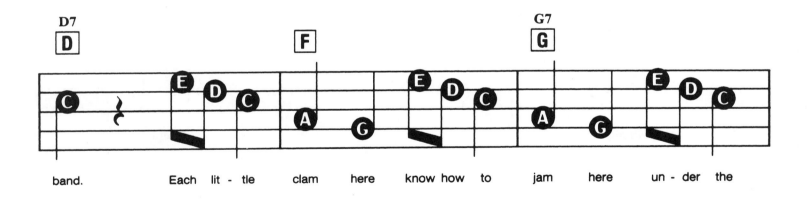

band. Each lit - tle clam here know how to jam here un - der the

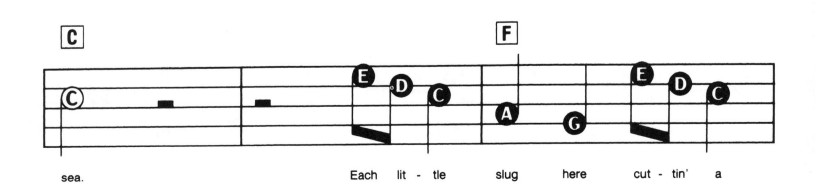

sea. Each lit - tle slug here cut - tin' a

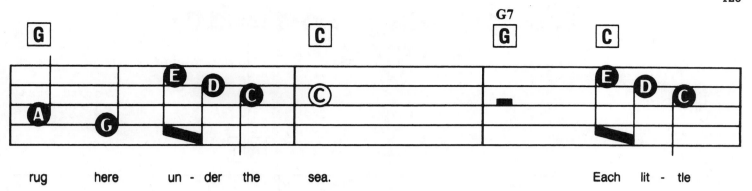

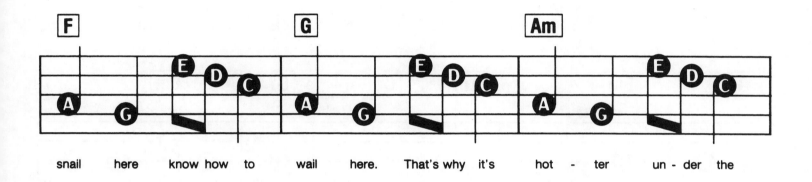

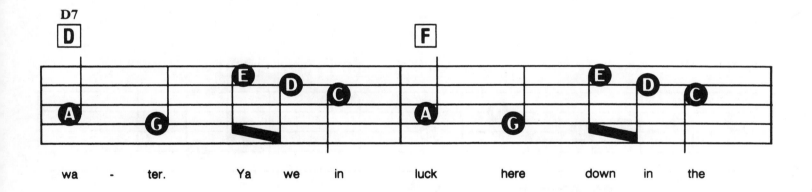

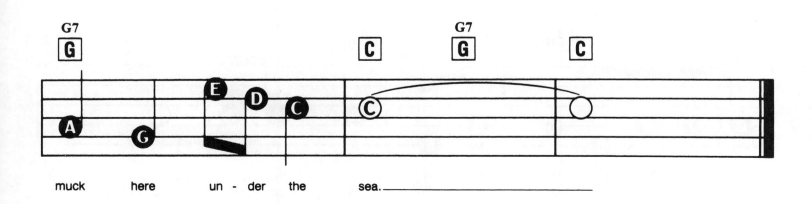

We Belong Together
from TOY STORY 3

Registration 2
Rhythm: Swing

Music and Lyrics by
Randy Newman

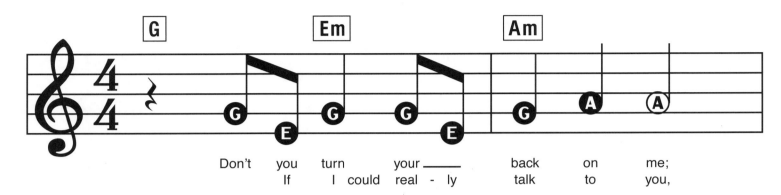

Don't you turn your _____ back on me;
If I could real - ly talk to you,

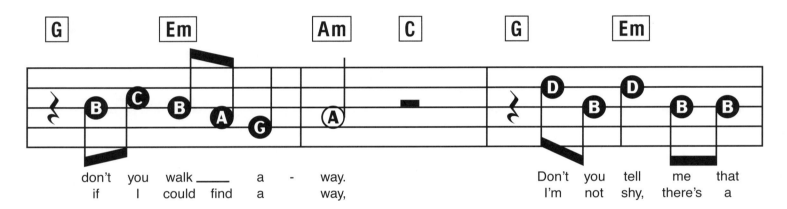

don't you walk _____ a - way.
if I could find a way,

Don't you tell me that
I'm not shy, there's a

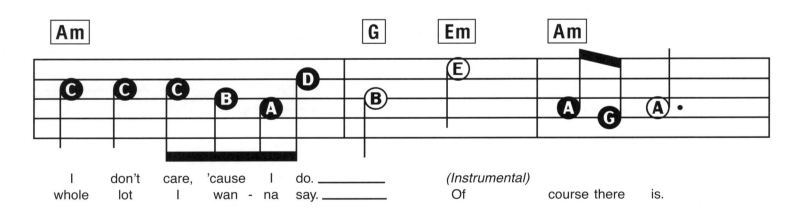

I don't care, 'cause I do. _____
whole lot I wan - na say. _____

(Instrumental)
Of course there is.

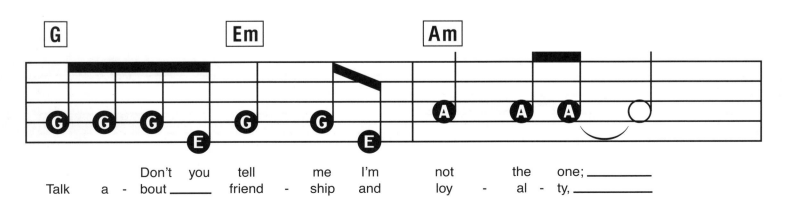

Don't you tell me I'm not the one; _____
Talk a - bout _____ friend - ship and loy - al - ty, _____

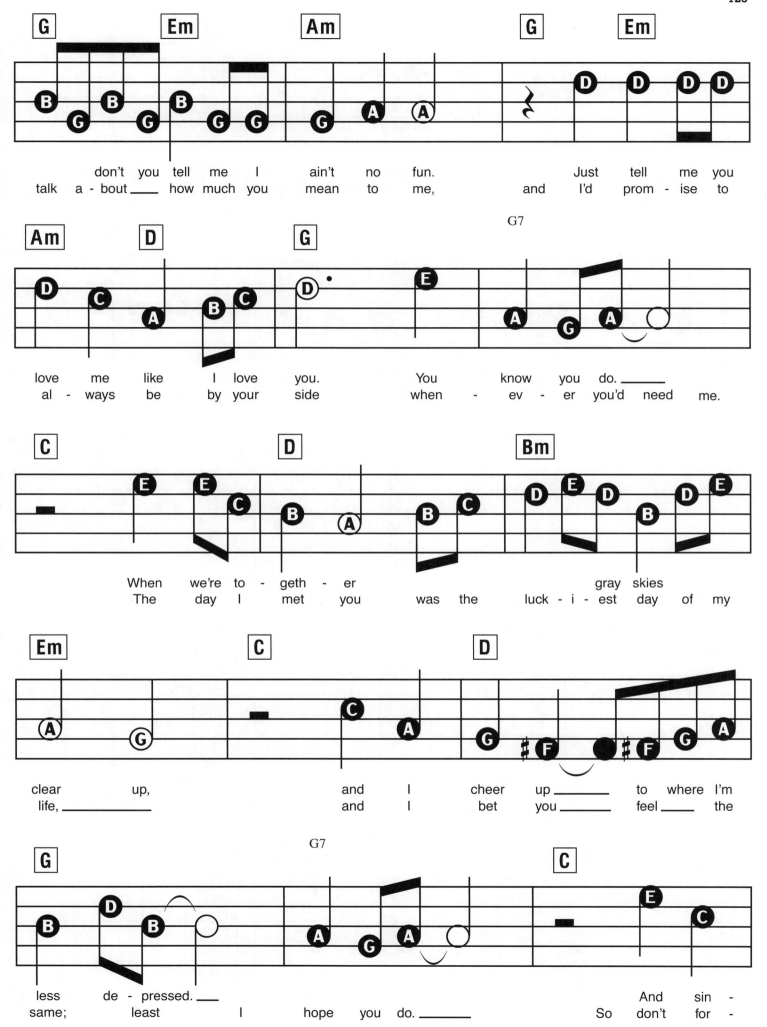

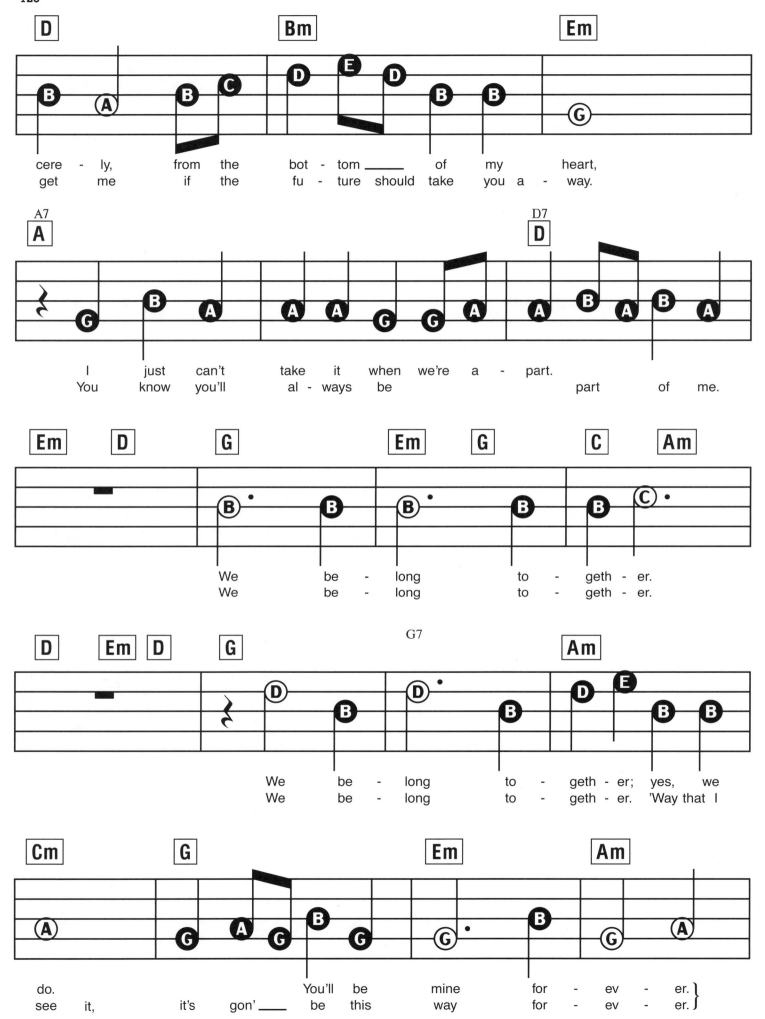

When She Loved Me

from TOY STORY 2

Registration 8
Rhythm: Ballad

Music and Lyrics by
Randy Newman

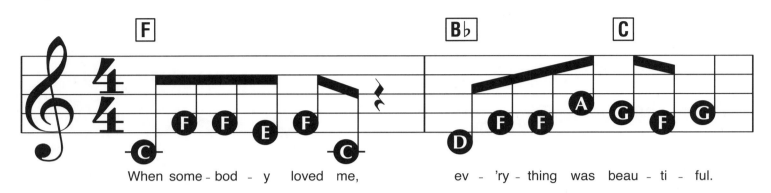

When some-bod-y loved me, ev-'ry-thing was beau-ti-ful.

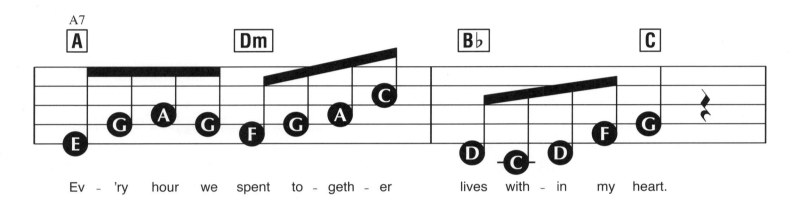

Ev-'ry hour we spent to-geth-er lives with-in my heart.

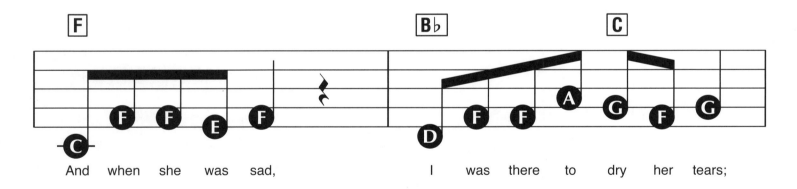

And when she was sad, I was there to dry her tears;

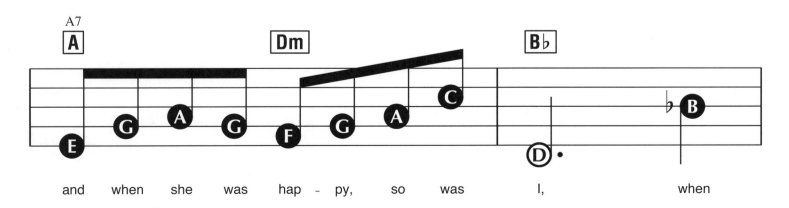

and when she was hap-py, so was I, when

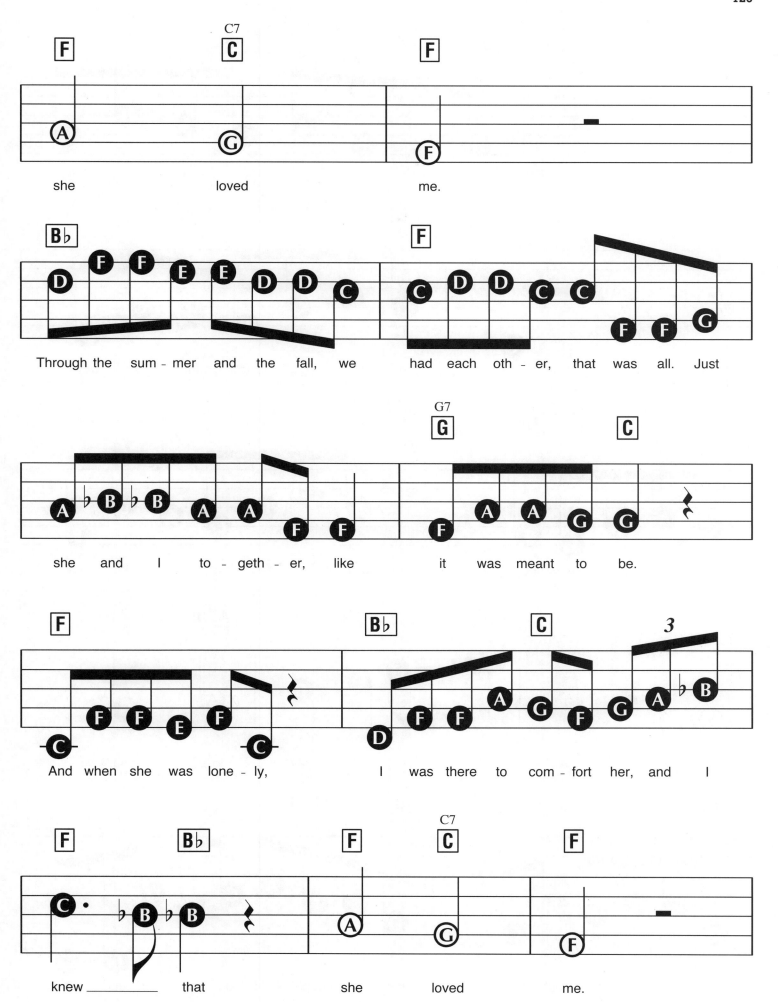

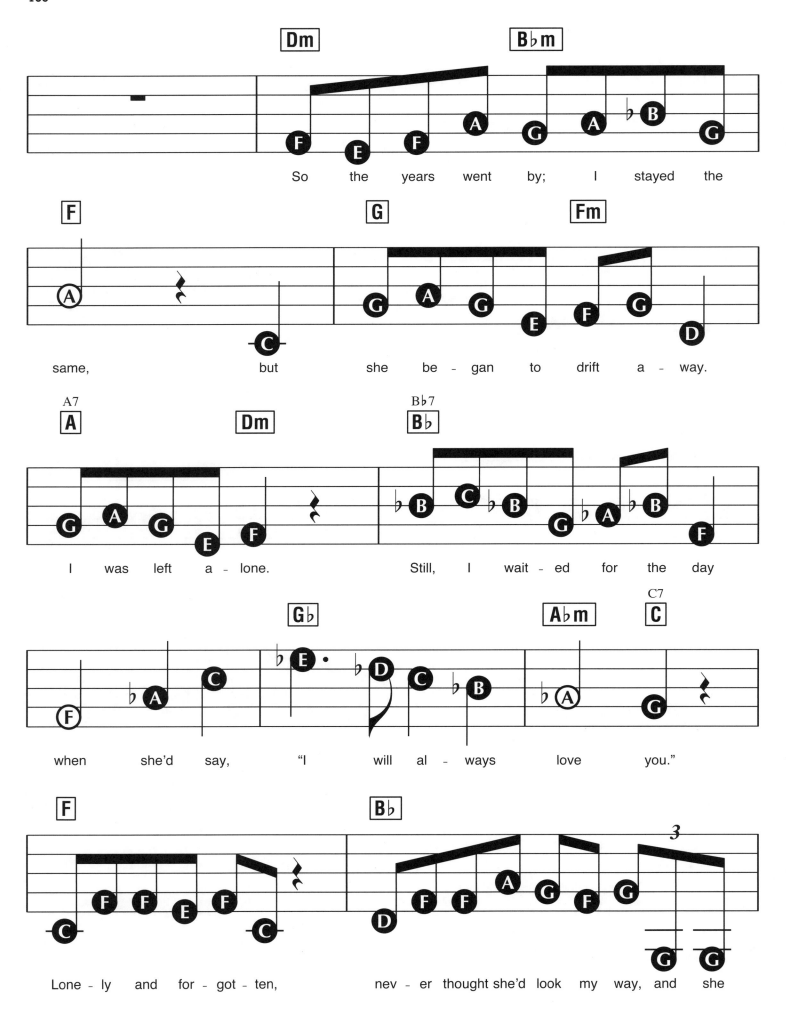

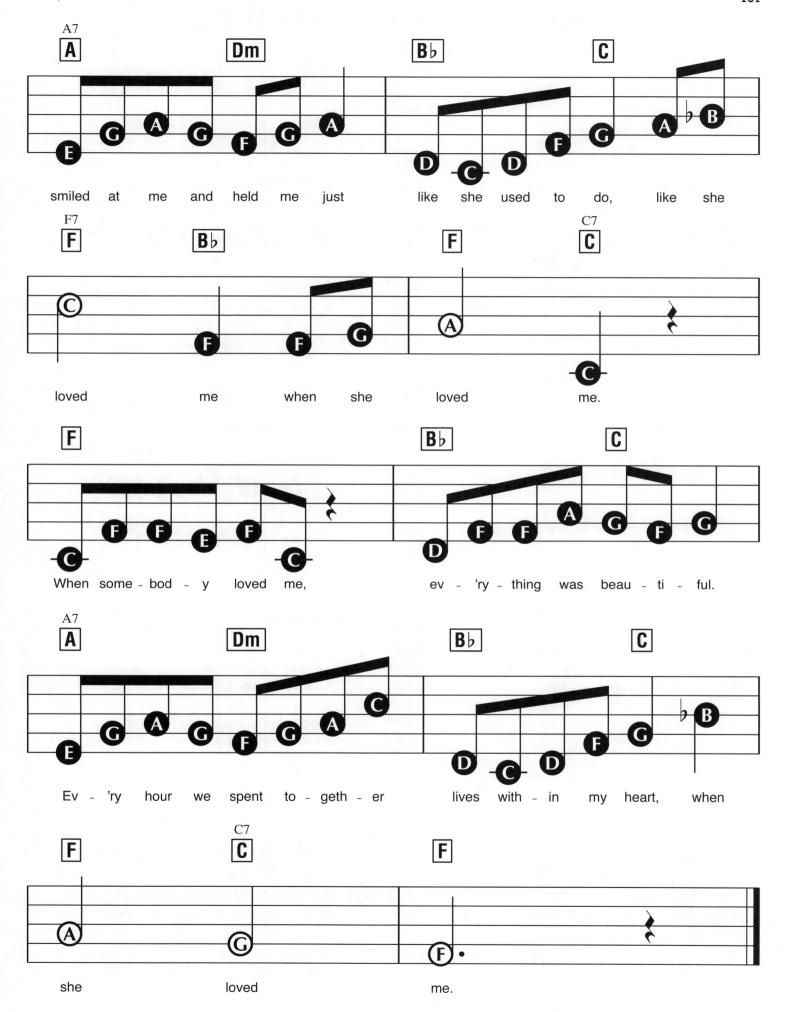

When Will My Life Begin?
from TANGLED

Registration 4
Rhythm: Fast Rock

Music by Alan Menken
Lyrics by Glenn Slater

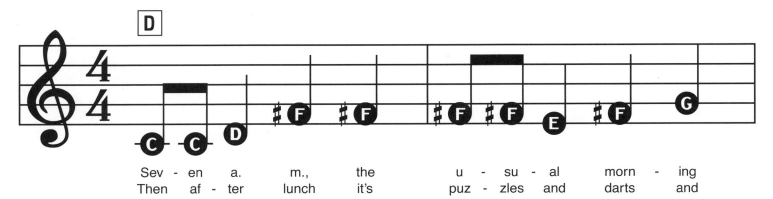

Sev - en a. m., the u - su - al morn - ing
Then af - ter lunch it's puz - zles and darts and

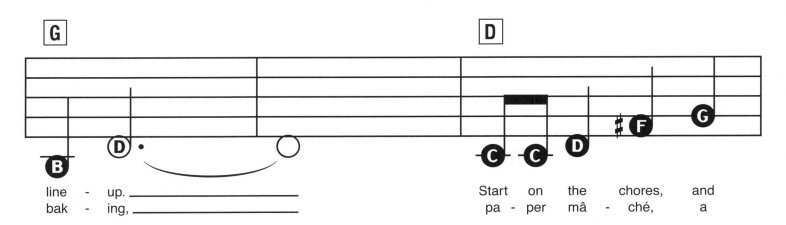

line - up. _____
bak - ing, _____

Start on the chores, and
pa - per mâ - ché, a

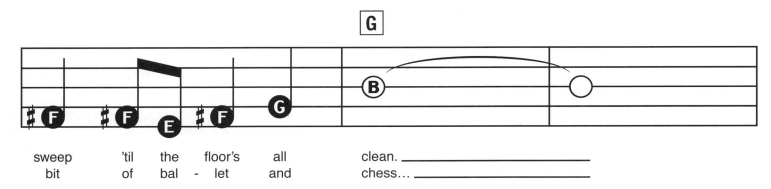

sweep 'til the floor's all clean. _____
bit of bal - let and chess... _____

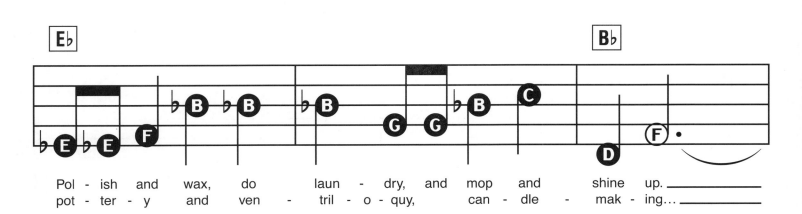

Pol - ish and wax, do laun - dry, and mop and shine up. _____
pot - ter - y and ven - tril - o - quy, can - dle - mak - ing... _____

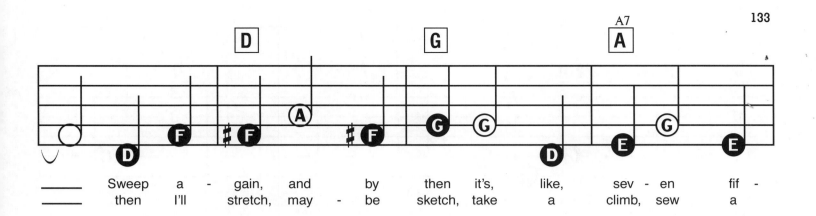

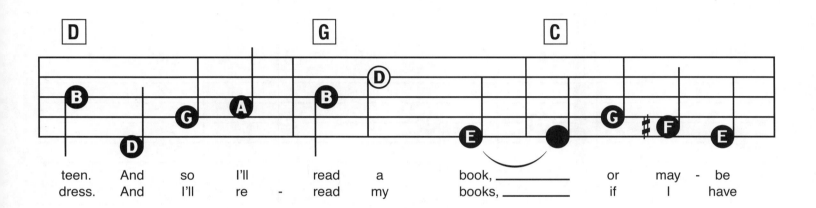

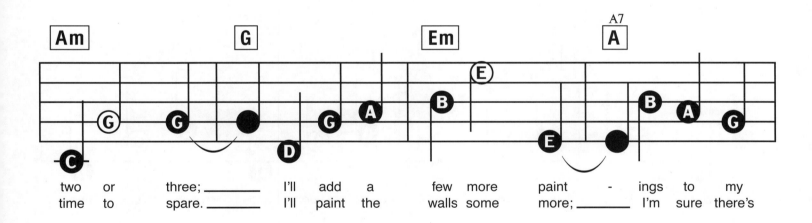

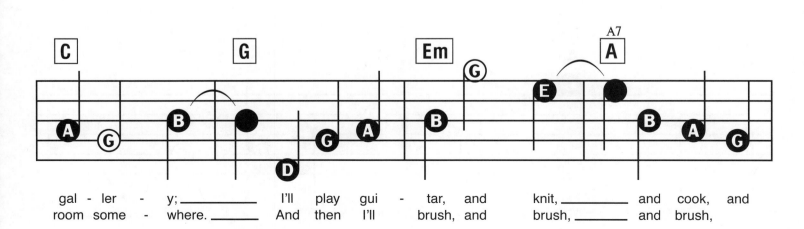

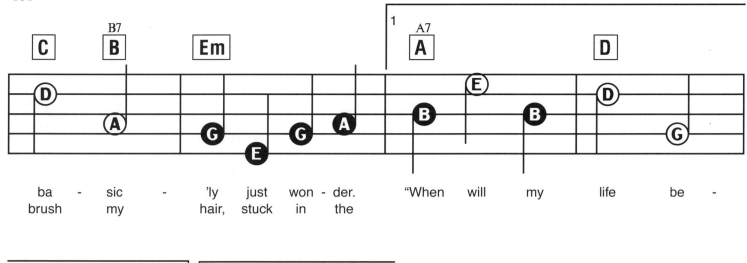

ba - sic - 'ly just won - der.
brush my hair, stuck in the

"When will my life be -

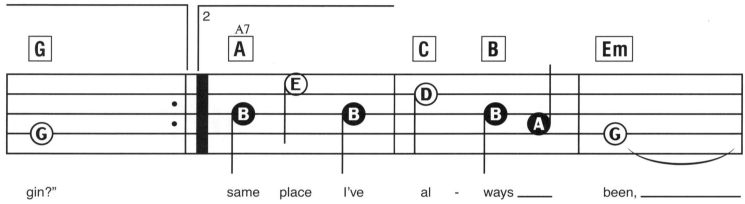

gin?"

same place I've al - ways ____ been, _____

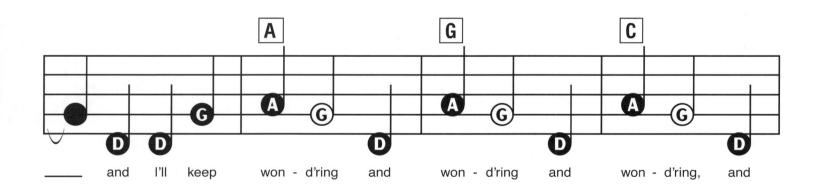

____ and I'll keep won - d'ring and won - d'ring and won - d'ring, and

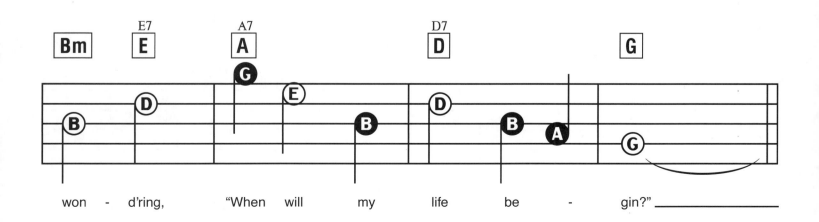

won - d'ring, "When will my life be - gin?" _____

Rhythm: None

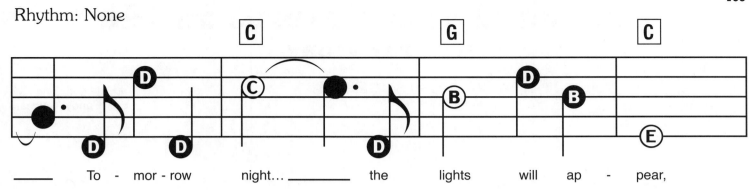

To - mor - row   night…_____   the   lights   will   ap - pear,

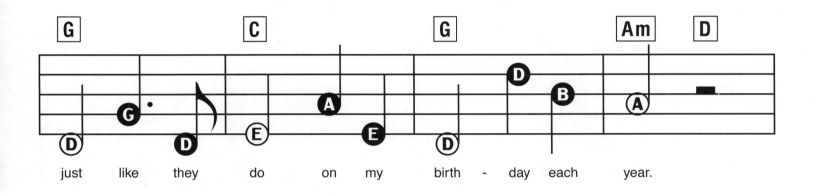

just   like   they   do   on   my   birth - day   each   year.

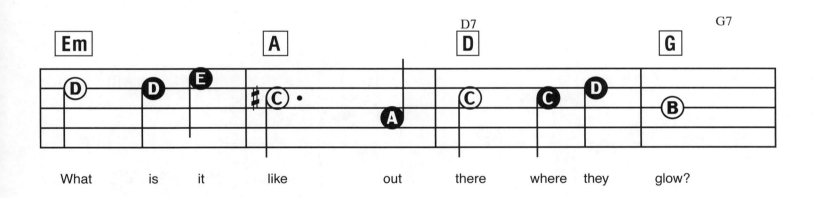

What   is   it   like   out   there   where   they   glow?

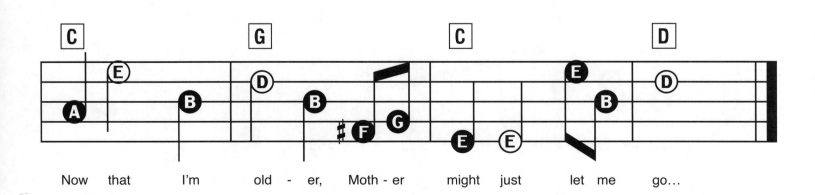

Now   that   I'm   old - er,   Moth - er   might   just   let   me   go…

You've Got a Friend in Me
from TOY STORY

Registration 7
Rhythm: Shuffle

Music and Lyrics by
Randy Newman

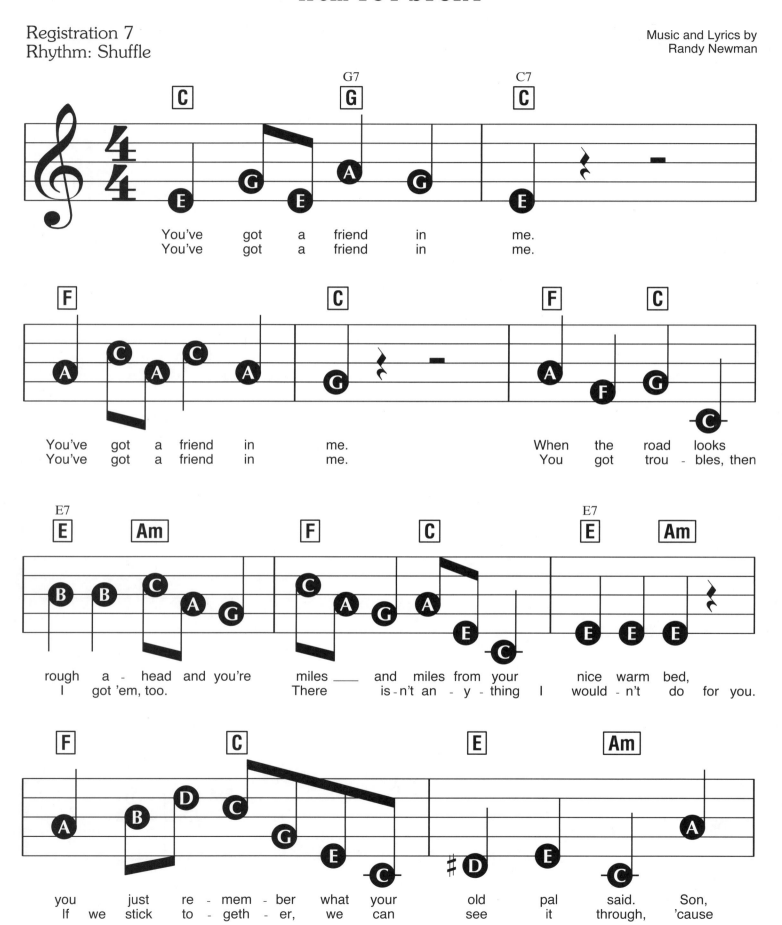

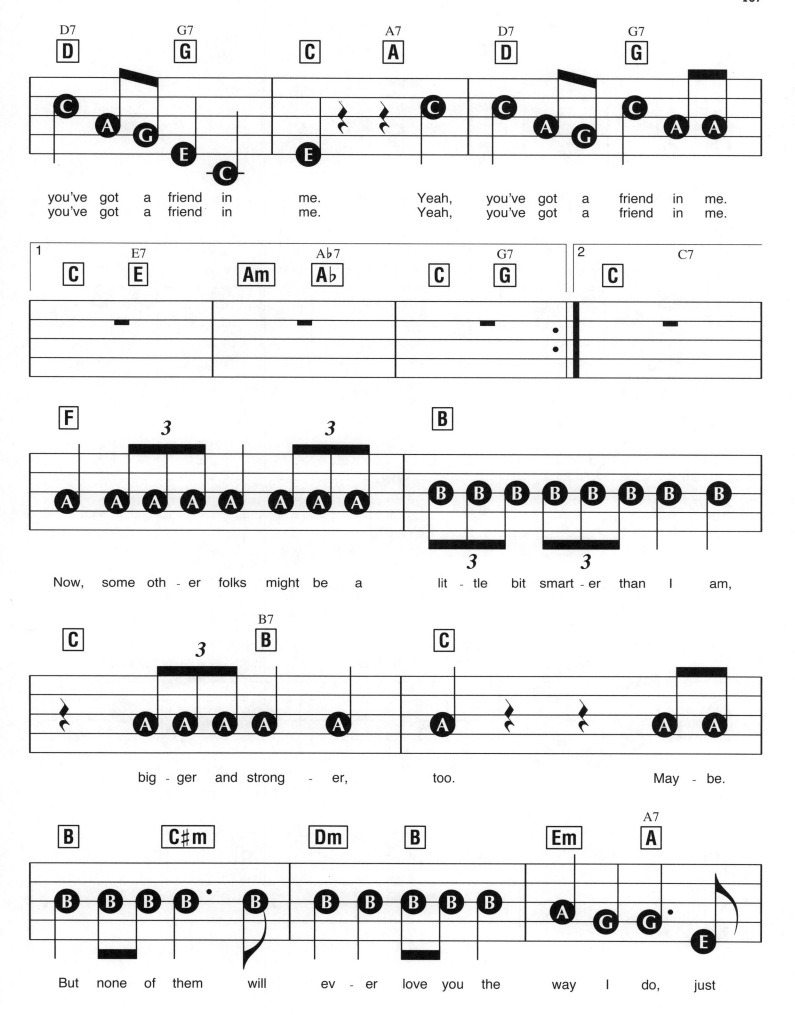

A Whole New World
from ALADDIN

Registration 1
Rhythm: Pops

Music by Alan Menken
Lyrics by Tim Rice

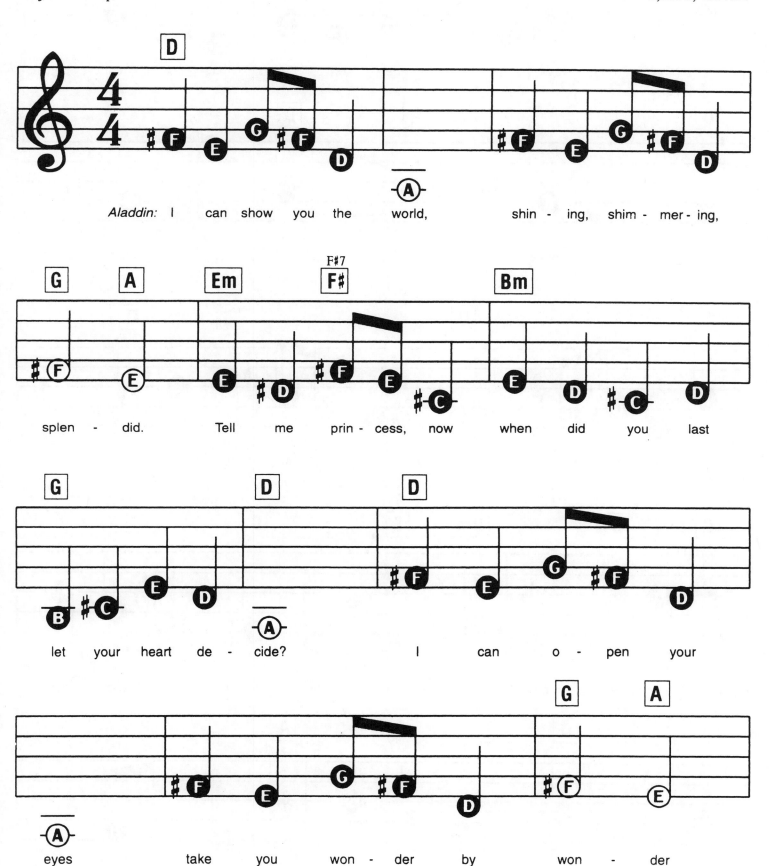

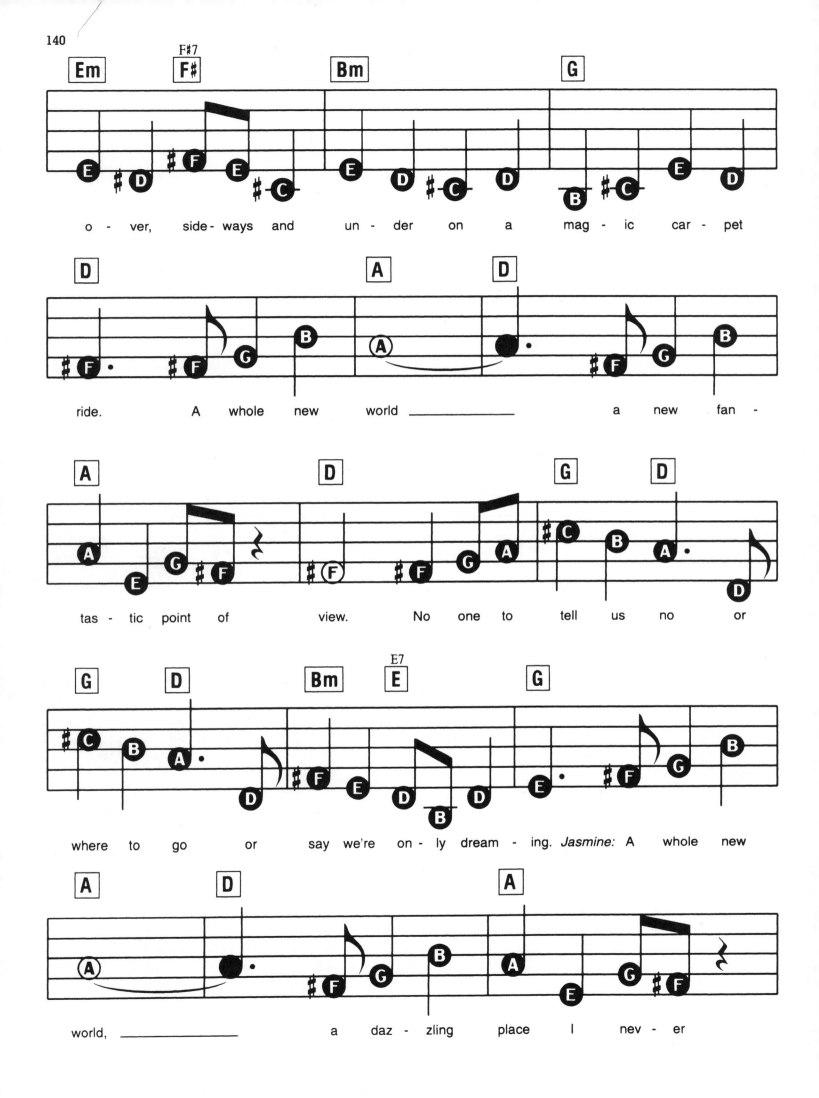

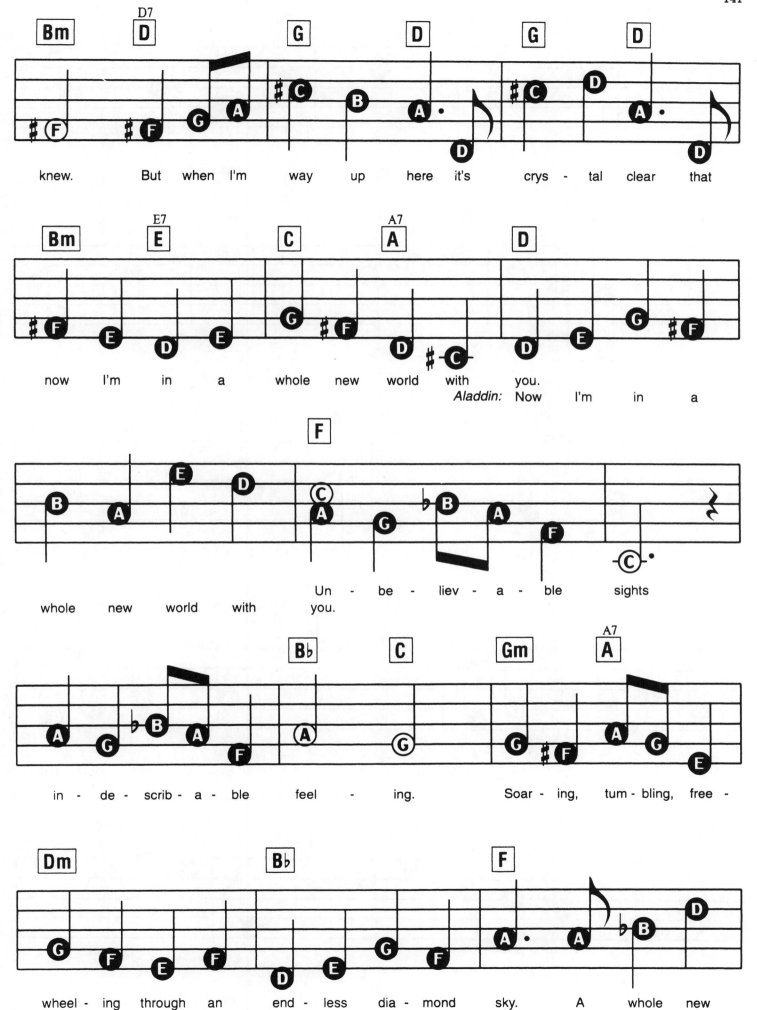

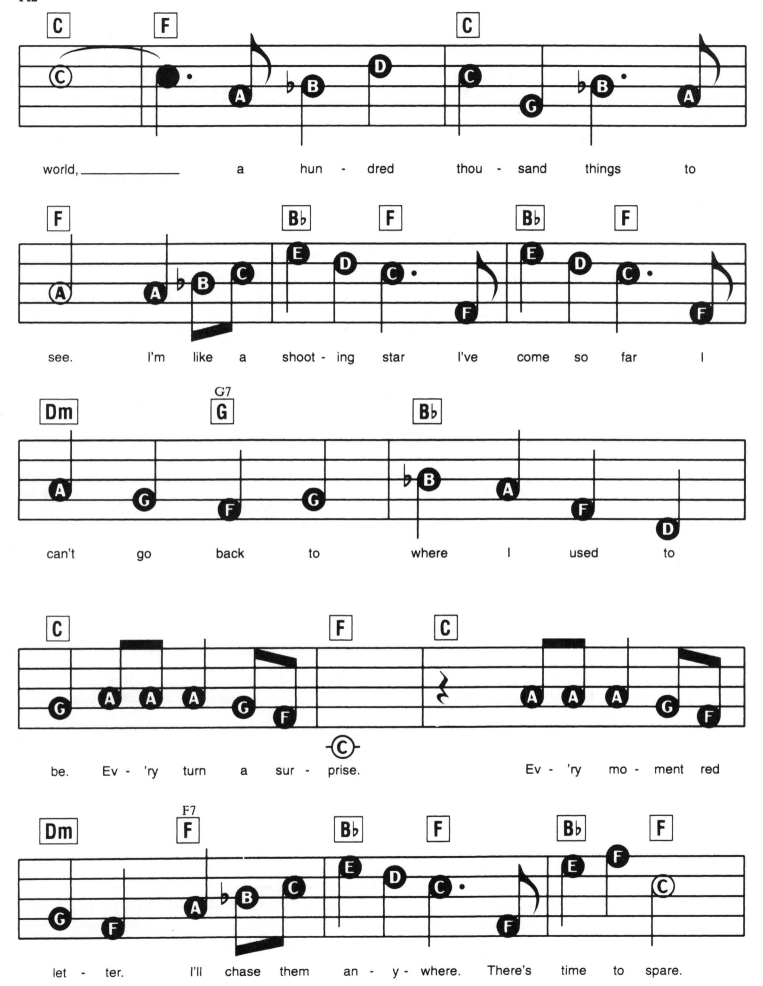

143

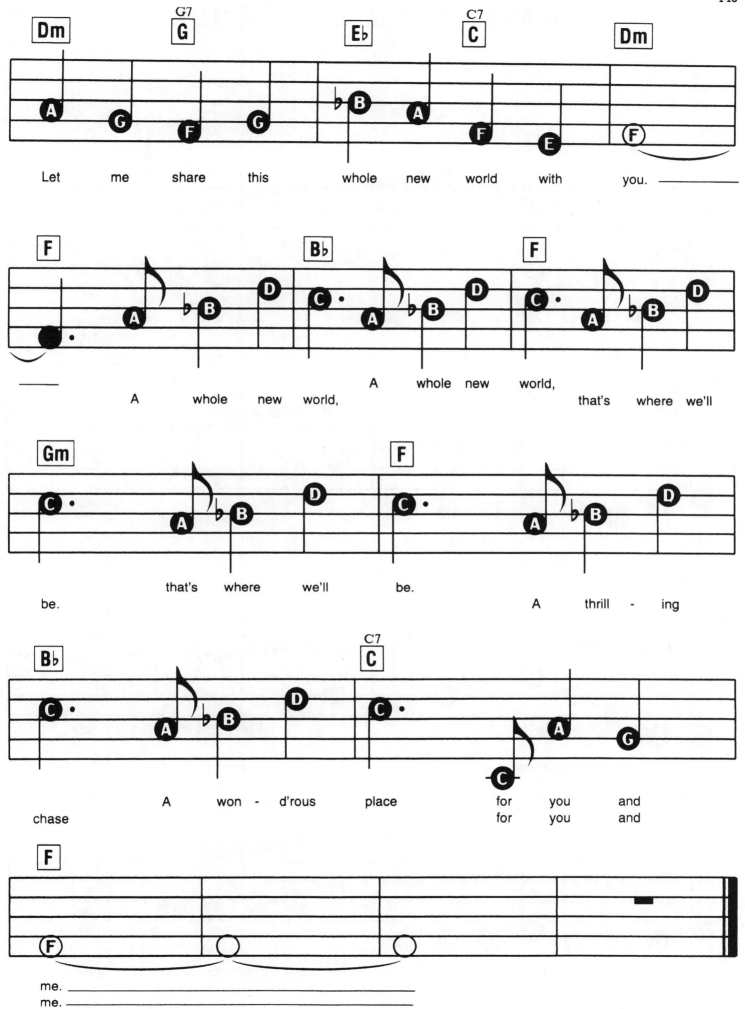

Written in the Stars
from AIDA

Registration 8
Rhythm: 8-Beat or Pops

Music by Alan Menken
Lyrics by Tim Rice

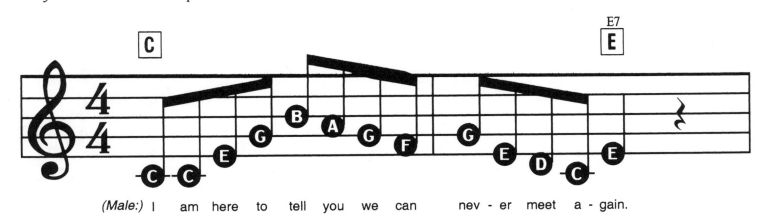

(Male:) I am here to tell you we can nev - er meet a - gain.

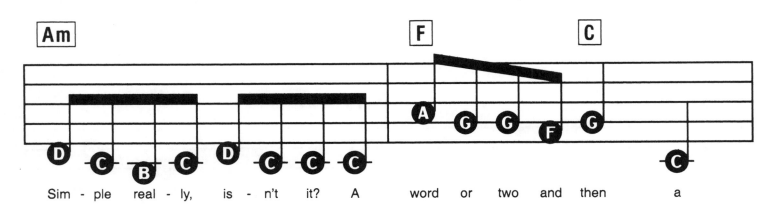

Sim - ple real - ly, is - n't it? A word or two and then a

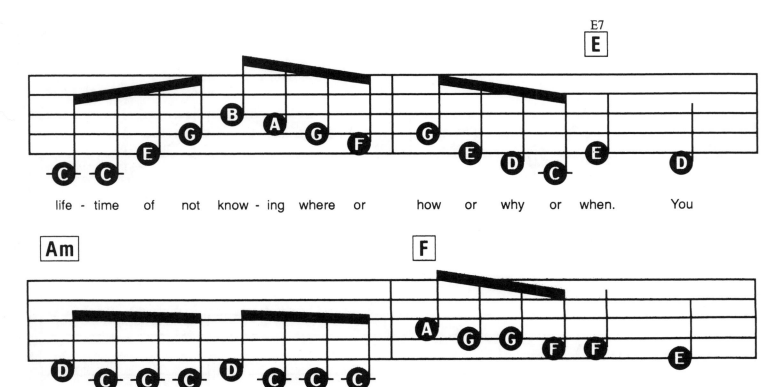

life - time of not know - ing where or how or why or when. You

think of me or speak of me or won - der what be - fell the

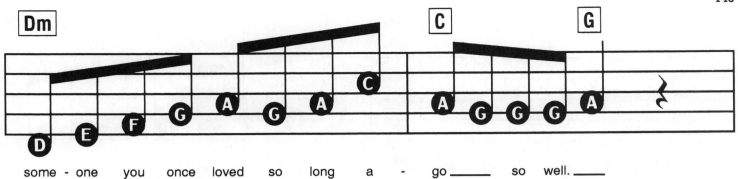

some - one you once loved so long a - go ___ so well. ___

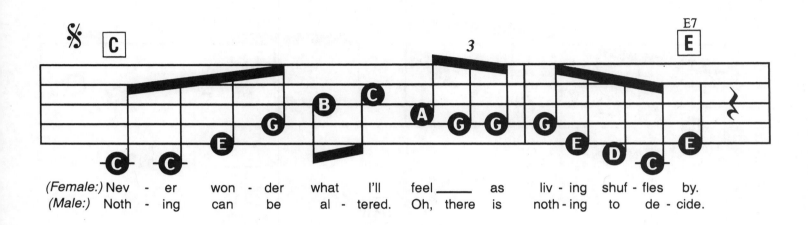

(Female:) Nev - er won - der what I'll feel ___ as liv - ing shuf - fles by.
(Male:) Noth - ing can be al - tered. Oh, there is noth - ing to de - cide.

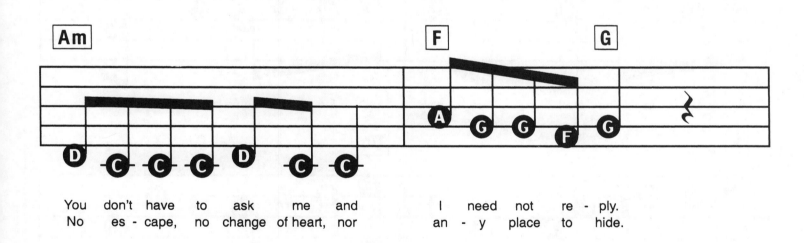

You don't have to ask me and I need not re - ply.
No es - cape, no change of heart, nor an - y place to hide.

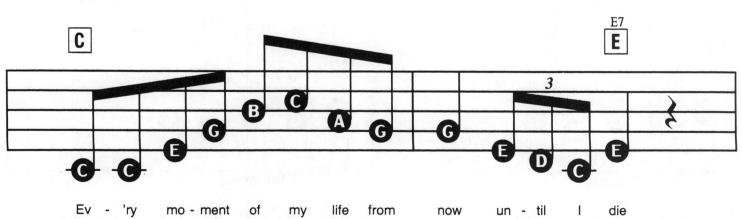

Ev - 'ry mo - ment of my life from now un - til I die
(Female:) You are all I'll ev - er want but this I am de - nied.

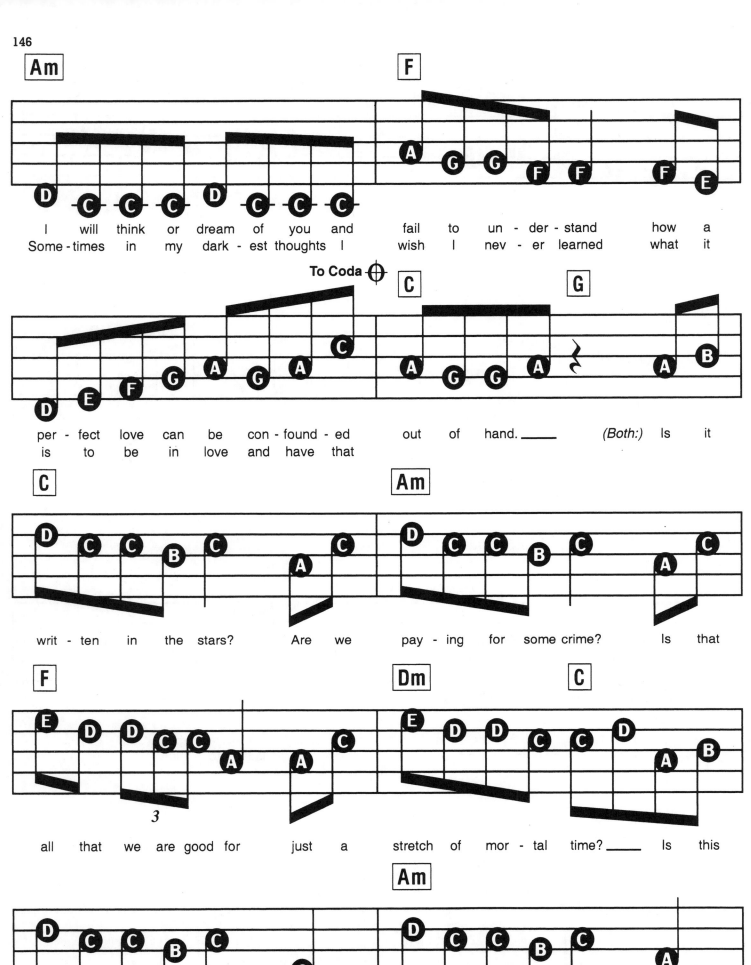

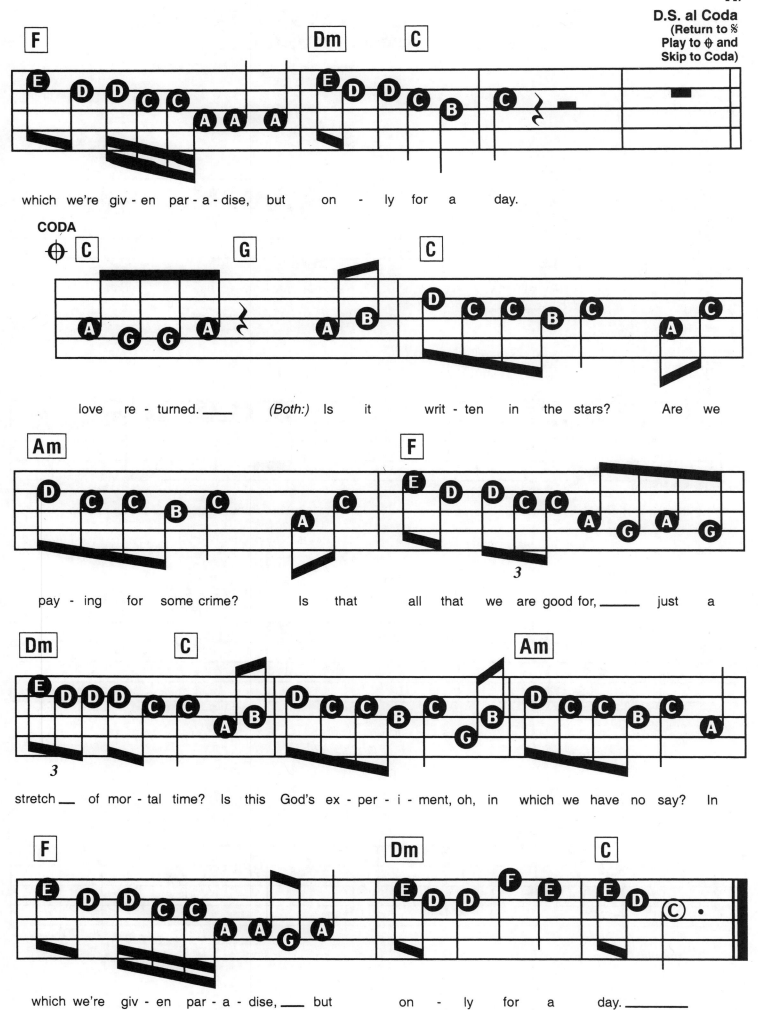

D.S. al Coda
(Return to %
Play to ⊕ and
Skip to Coda)

which we're giv - en par - a - dise, but on - ly for a day.

CODA

love re - turned. ____ *(Both:)* Is it writ - ten in the stars? Are we

pay - ing for some crime? Is that all that we are good for, _____ just a

stretch __ of mor - tal time? Is this God's ex - per - i - ment, oh, in which we have no say? In

which we're giv - en par - a - dise, __ but on - ly for a day. _____

You Are the Music in Me
from HIGH SCHOOL MUSICAL 2

Registration 2
Rhythm: Dance or Rock

Words and Music by
Jamie Houston

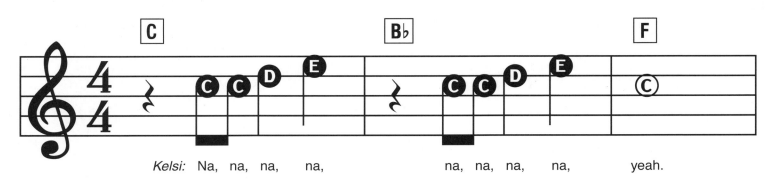

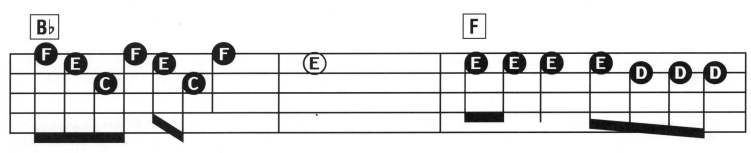

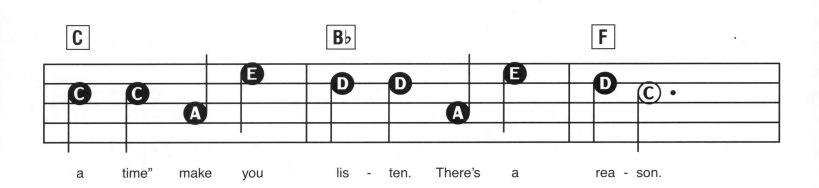

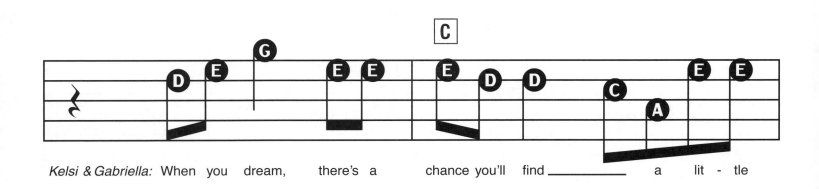

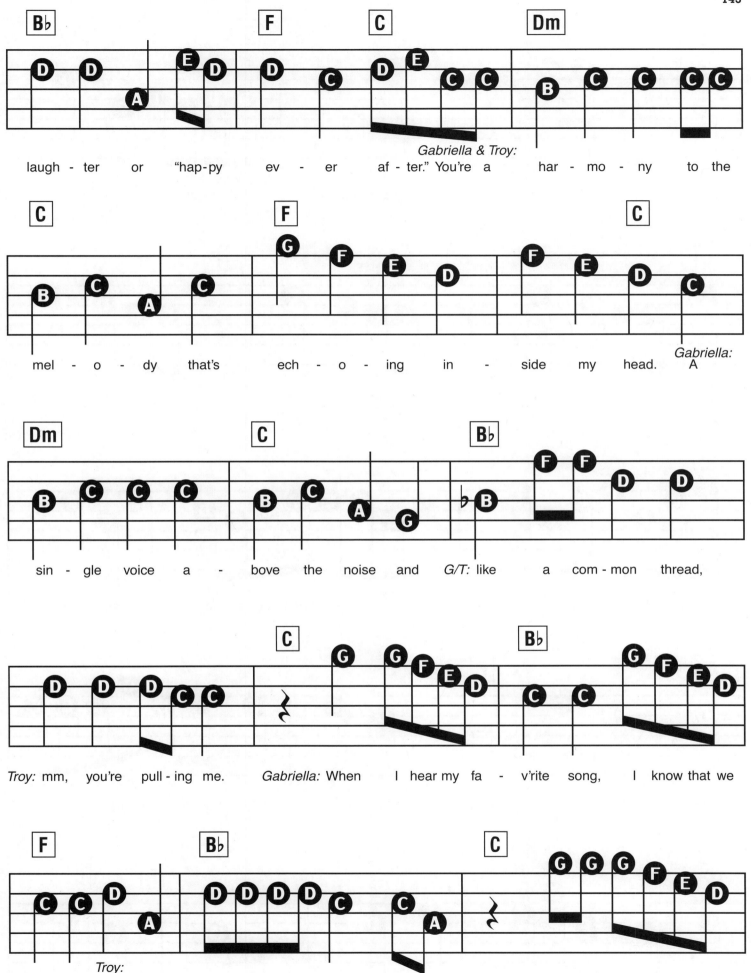

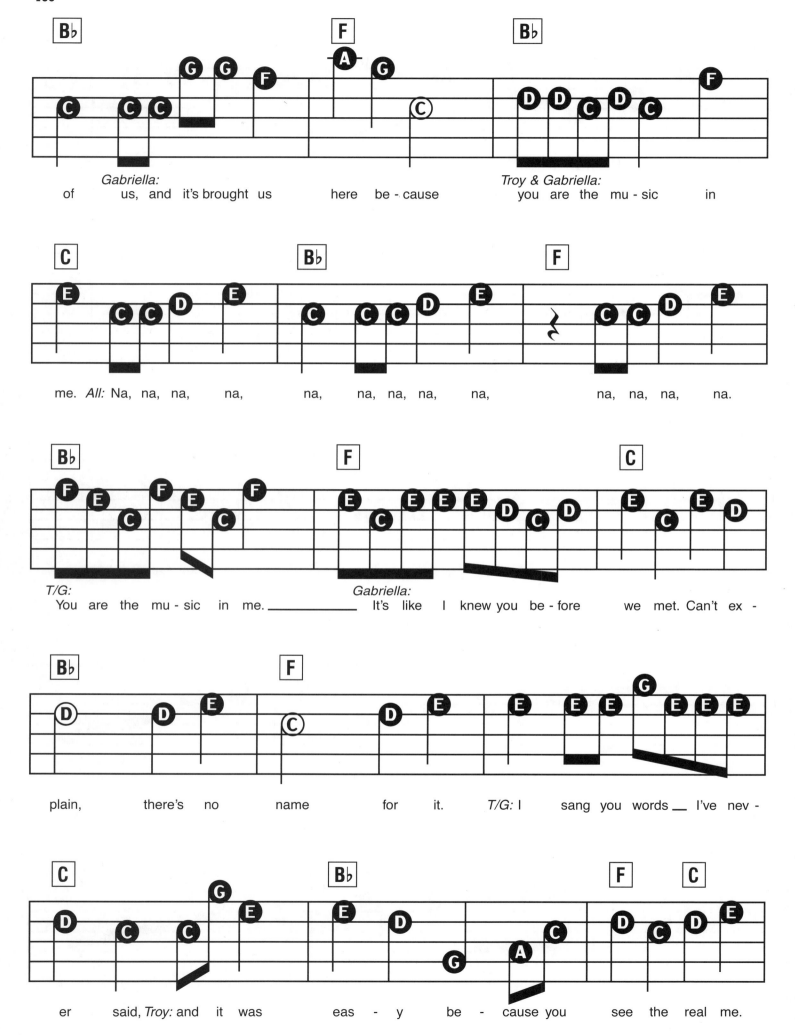

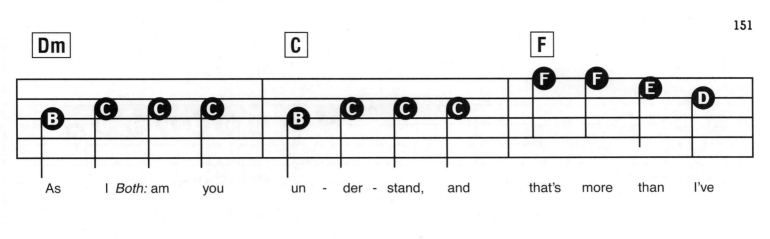

As I *Both:* am you un - der - stand, and that's more than I've

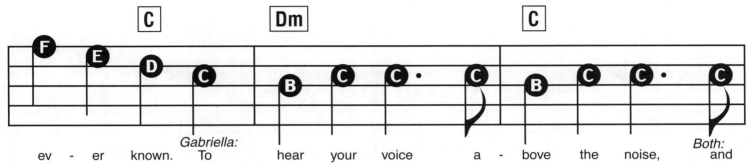

ev - er known. *Gabriella:* To hear your voice a - bove the noise, *Both:* and

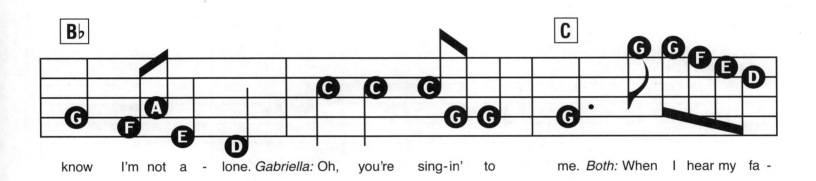

know I'm not a - lone. *Gabriella:* Oh, you're sing-in' to me. *Both:* When I hear my fa -

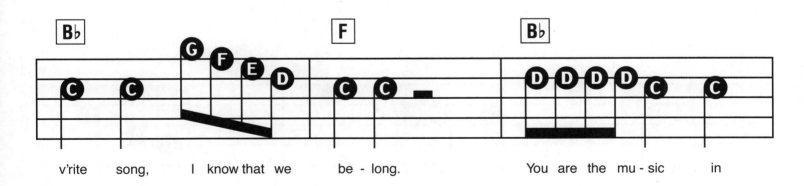

v'rite song, I know that we be - long. You are the mu - sic in

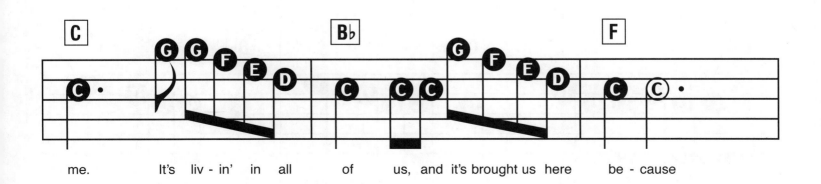

me. It's liv - in' in all of us, and it's brought us here be - cause

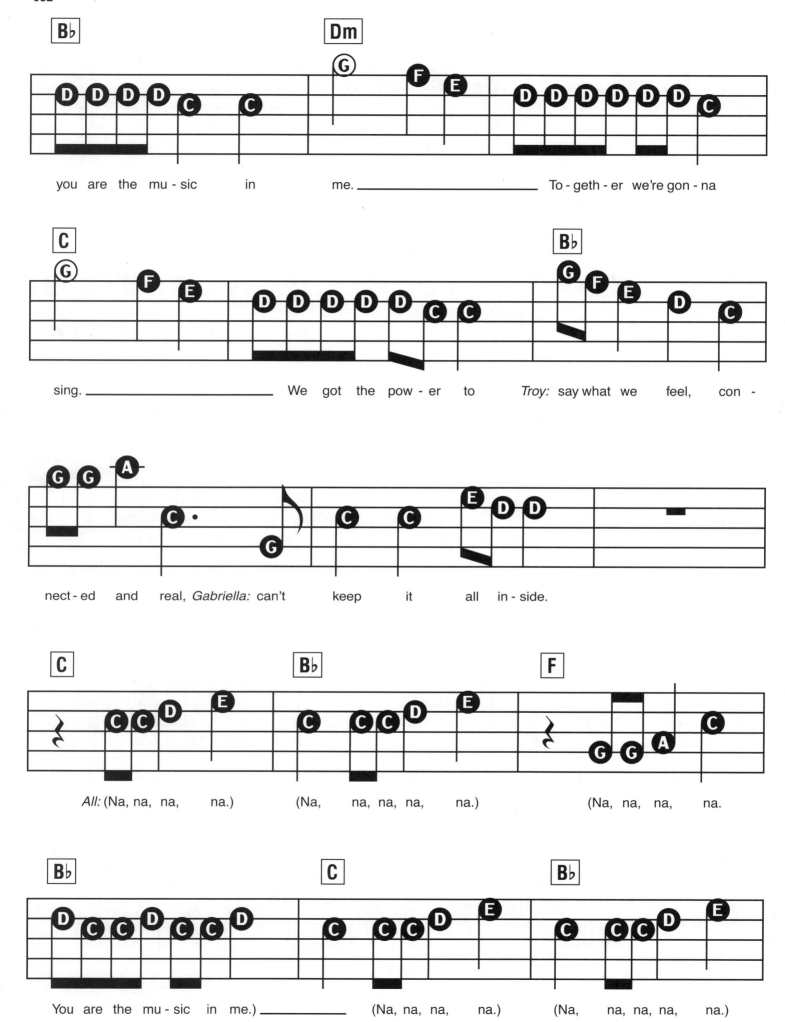

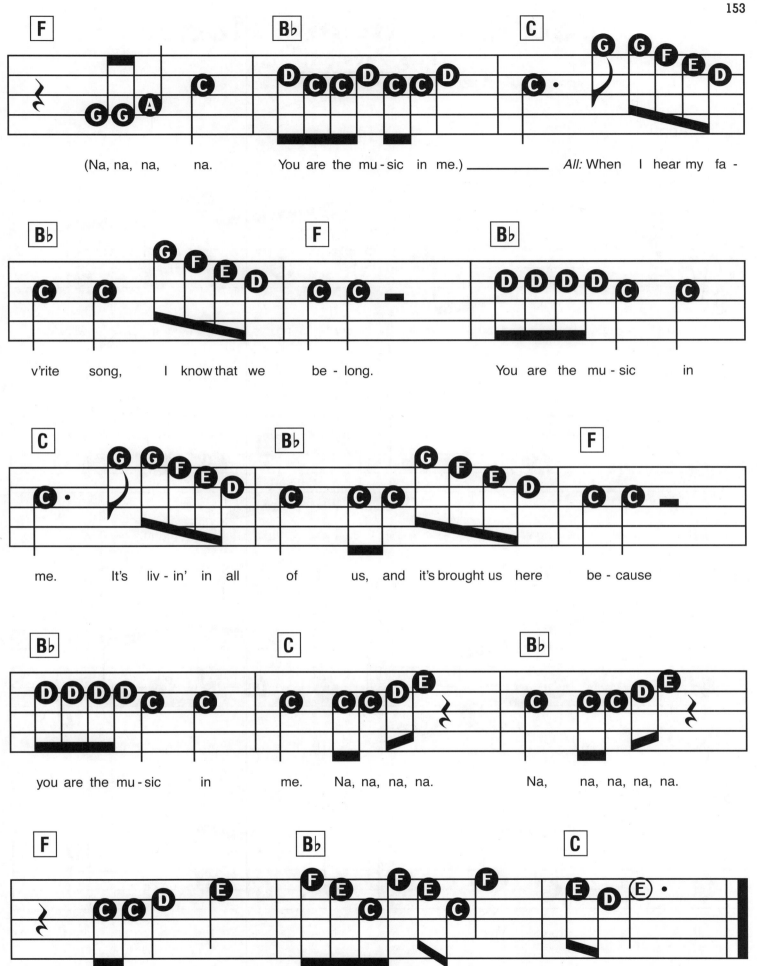

You'll Be in My Heart

(Pop Version)
from TARZAN™

Registration 1
Rhythm: Rock or Pops

Words and Music by
Phil Collins

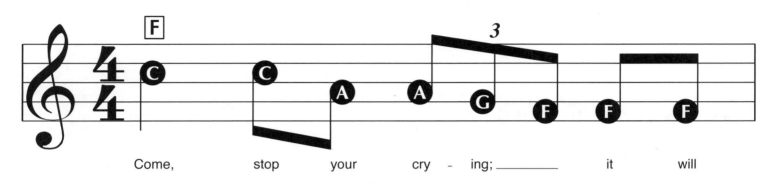

Come, stop your cry - ing; _____ it will

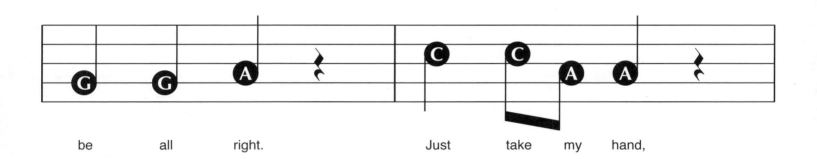

be all right. Just take my hand,

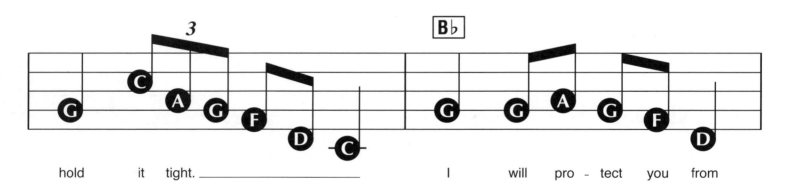

hold it tight. _____ I will pro - tect you from

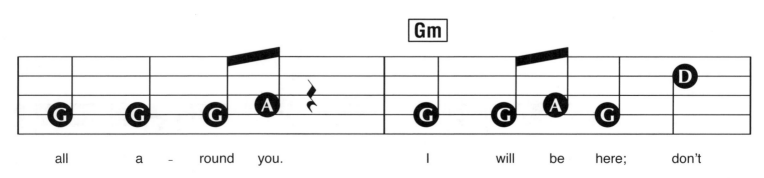

all a - round you. I will be here; don't

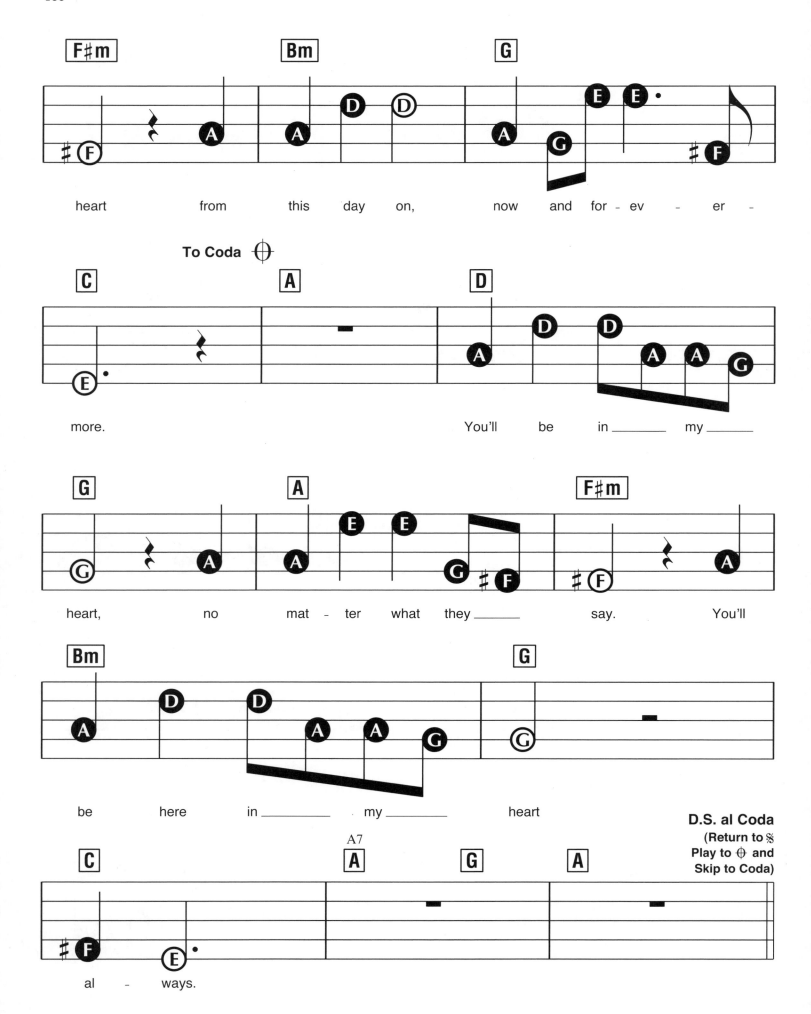

CODA

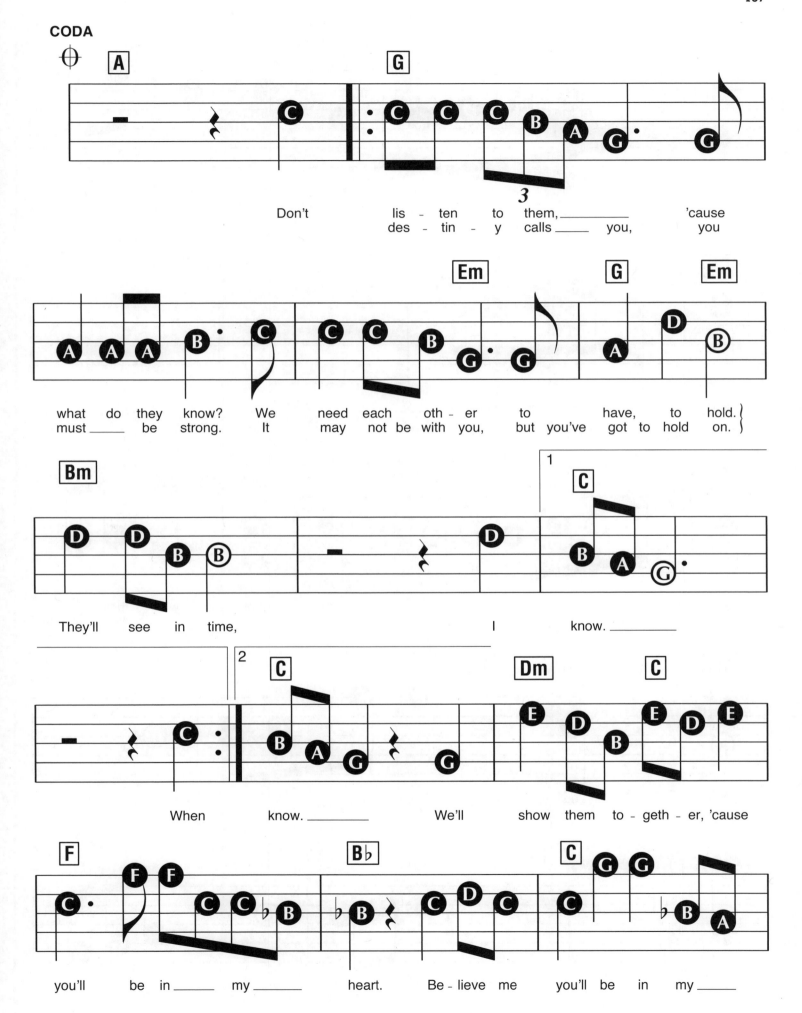

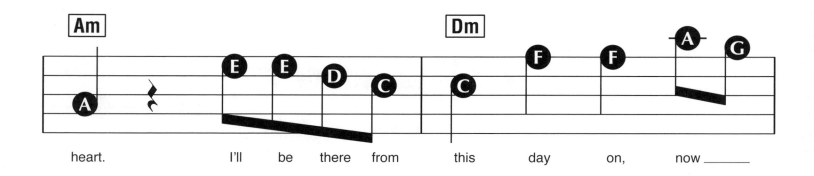

heart.   I'll   be   there   from   this   day   on,   now _____

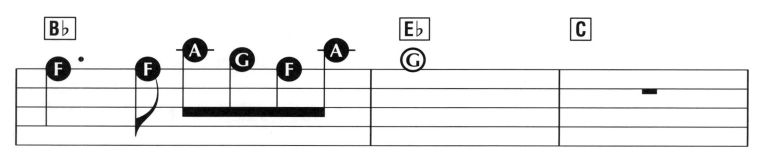

and   for - ev - er - more. _____

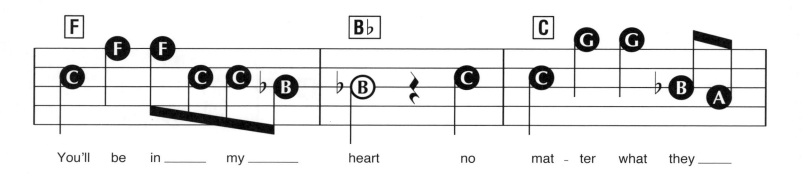

You'll   be   in _____ my _____ heart   no   mat - ter   what   they _____

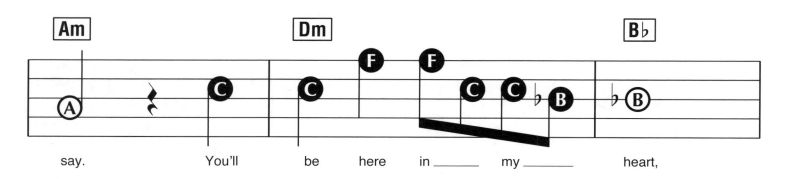

say.   You'll   be   here   in _____ my _____ heart,

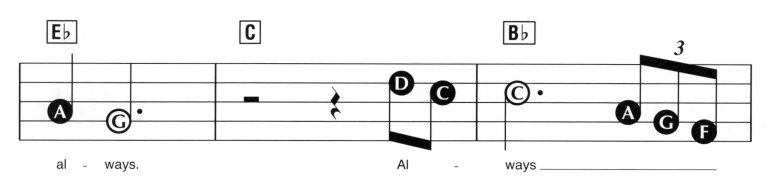

al - ways.   Al - ways _____

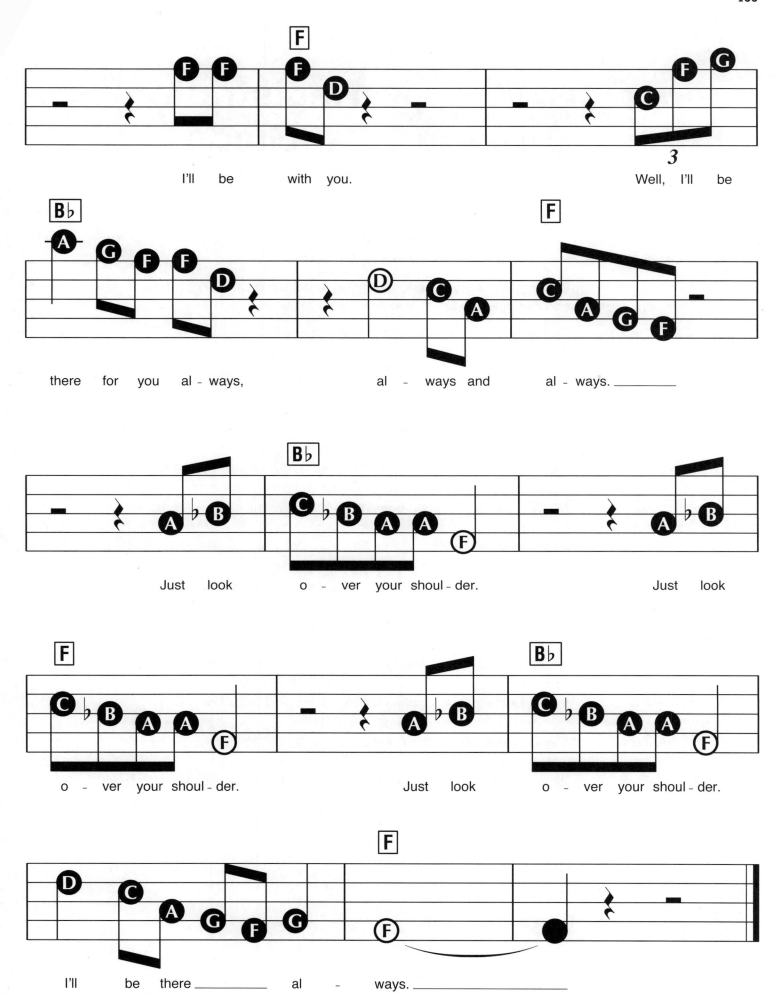

Registration Guide

- Match the Registration number on the song to the corresponding numbered category below. Select and activate an instrumental sound available on your instrument.

- Choose an automatic rhythm appropriate to the mood and style of the song. (Consult your Owner's Guide for proper operation of automatic rhythm features.)

- Adjust the tempo and volume controls to comfortable settings.

Registration

1	Mellow	Flutes, Clarinet, Oboe, Flugel Horn, Trombone, French Horn, Organ Flutes
2	Ensemble	Brass Section, Sax Section, Wind Ensemble, Full Organ, Theater Organ
3	Strings	Violin, Viola, Cello, Fiddle, String Ensemble, Pizzicato, Organ Strings
4	Guitars	Acoustic/Electric Guitars, Banjo, Mandolin, Dulcimer, Ukulele, Hawaiian Guitar
5	Mallets	Vibraphone, Marimba, Xylophone, Steel Drums, Bells, Celesta, Chimes
6	Liturgical	Pipe Organ, Hand Bells, Vocal Ensemble, Choir, Organ Flutes
7	Bright	Saxophones, Trumpet, Mute Trumpet, Synth Leads, Jazz/Gospel Organs
8	Piano	Piano, Electric Piano, Honky Tonk Piano, Harpsichord, Clavi
9	Novelty	Melodic Percussion, Wah Trumpet, Synth, Whistle, Kazoo, Perc. Organ
10	Bellows	Accordion, French Accordion, Mussette, Harmonica, Pump Organ, Bagpipes